THE LIFE WE CLAIM

THE LIFE
WE CLAIM

THE APOSTLES' CREED
FOR PREACHING
TEACHING
AND WORSHIP

JAMES C. HOWELL

ABINGDON PRESS / *Nashville*

THE LIFE WE CLAIM
THE APOSTLES' CREED FOR PREACHING, TEACHING, AND WORSHIP

This book is printed on acid-free paper.

Library of Congress Cataloging-in-Publication Data

Howell, James C., 1955-
   The life we claim : the Apostles' Creed for preaching, teaching, and worship / James C. Howell.
      p. cm.
   ISBN 0-687-49353-6 (alk. paper)
   1. Apostles' Creed. I. Title.

BT993.3.H69 2005
238'.11—dc22

2005016444

05 06 07 08 09 10 11 12 13 14—10 9 8 7 6 5 4 3 2 1
MANUFACTURED IN THE UNITED STATES OF AMERICA

To Craig and Jason

CONTENTS

PREFACE

Many Christians have stood on cue in worship to repeat the Apostles' Creed, words they learned years ago, but have never thought much about them. Many churches have decided that the words of the Creed do not appeal to modern consumers and may even repel some of the very people we hope to reel in. Many so-called seekers have poked their heads into the Church, unsure what exactly would be offered: a satisfying experience? Intellectual content? Something old? Something fresh?

The Apostles' Creed is spoken, in unison, perhaps thoughtlessly, or perhaps with the solid substance that is manifest when a couple parts in the morning with a kiss that is little bit perfunctory but bears witness to something deep and large. To reflect upon the depth of the repeated kiss is a good idea, and we may be sure that a close examination of the historic Apostles' Creed will more than repay the effort. We want to know what we really believe, and why. We need to know if there is anything substantive to hang on to in the Church. We need to ask questions, and to be asked questions, to test our minds and souls, to grow in a kind of spirituality that is not just free-floating, but coming from someplace, and going to someplace that is significant.

Our time with the Apostles' Creed is richer if we explore these matters together, in worship, in classes, in common study and prayer. Originally, the Creed was designed for worship, and that is where the Creed is most frequently experienced today. A church family can discover a shared identity, and grow into a more zealous mission together by working through the Creed. This book unfolds into a roadmap for Christians to think carefully, pray diligently, and live faithfully around the Creed. It can be read solo, but it can also function as a book for common study; it offers suggested sermons (deeper reflections) and worship resources, which could be used in many settings, but with particular benefit in the actual worship life of the congregation.

Two Challenges

Should you as an individual or your church as a body delve into this series, you must know that a pair of dissonant melodies will be playing in the background. Many walk in the door with in an anti-creedal mood: "I do not trust ancient, established authorities. I want to believe on my own. I am the one who will decide for myself." This mood is not random, but has fermented because established authorities have let us down quite a few times. We will need to help the skeptics see that the Creed was not birthed in a bullying, dictatorial way. The Creed was the focused, worshipful expression of people whose lives had been totally transformed by the Bible and by the risen Jesus Christ. The Creed's words are not windows with the shutters pulled down tightly, but windows thrown open into the very heart of life with God.

Others walk in the door in a pro-creedal mood, but misconstruing the Creed as some sort of litmus test to be rigidly applied: "If you do not give assent to every word of our dogma, if you raise even faint questions, you are not worthy of the Kingdom of God." But the Creed was not designed as a massive stone wall to keep out unbelievers. In fact, there is a "blessed spareness"[1] in the Creed, pushing no theory of sin, no theory of the meaning of Jesus' death, no prescription for how the Church should be structured. There is room in the Creed for many kinds of Christians, and there is room in the Creed for questions.

About This Book

How will we explore the Creed and its questions? This book provides brief, digestible lessons of roughly six hundred words each. You may simply read the lessons, or you may wish to use them in classes. You could print them in the church newsletter or bulletin—and in this modern, technological era, you would be wise to e-mail these to the congregation through the week in preparation for the coming Sunday. More and more churches are not just throwing up Web sites, but gifting people's e-mail boxes with inspirational, educational lessons. You'll have to collect addresses and promise the recipients you will not ask for anything except a little time and interest. The lessons must be personal, emanating from the senior pastor herself, or the teaching pastor himself.

In the appendix, you will find detailed suggestions for music to use in worship. Remember: the Creed was sung in worship before it was analyzed and dissected in the classroom! We cannot believe in God or think about God somehow prior to worship; if we have faith or think faithfully, it is because we have met God in regular worship.[2] A worship series on the Apostles' Creed could extend over an indefinite period of time, or it could pass swiftly. But you probably need a minimum of ten weeks to touch on the major theses. This book falls into fourteen sections. Depending on the time of year, a series on the Creed can dovetail beautifully into the Christian year. When I did this series, we began the Sunday after the New Year—a good time, as people are fresh and motivated, in many places it's too cold to spend much time outdoors, and resolutions are still dancing in people's heads. Lent commenced right at the point of "He shall come to judge," "the forgiveness of sins" landed on Palm Sunday, and Easter culminated it all with "the resurrection of the body." The sermons included can be read as merely inspirational, or as exemplary of how to preach on the Creed. Dozens of sermons could be hatched on each article of the Creed: but know that at least one church in Charlotte, North Carolina, heard and received these with enthusiasm.

I should thank many who have helped with this project. Kevin Turner, a superbly talented young church musician, prepared the lists of worship resources in the appendix. Jill Reddig of Abingdon Press continues to be a wonderfully encouraging presence throughout the publication process. Jason Byassee and Ben Witherington read the full manuscript and offered many helpful suggestions. My secretary, Nancy Pryor, has been of tremendous support, as have been the members of Myers Park United Methodist Church, who first walked through the Creed with me in the winter and spring of 2003. My favorite member of Myers Park is the one I met and married in that very church; with this book as with all the others Lisa has been the biggest fan a writer could ever hope to have.

And so we begin, with four introductory lessons before we walk our way through the Creed itself.

Notes

1. Luke Timothy Johnson, *The Creed: What Christians Believe and Why It Matters* (New York: Doubleday, 2003), 282.

2. Stanley Hauerwas is determined to "defeat the dreaded 'and'—as in 'theology and worship'" (in *In Good Company: The Church as Polis* [Notre Dame: University of Notre Dame, 1995], 155), which also demeans itself into a more daunting "and" between worship (or theology) and ethics. The preacher need never be confused about the relationship between theology and preaching if she remembers that theology happens in the discipline of the liturgy or not at all.

Chapter One

INTRODUCTION TO THE APOSTLES' CREED

LESSON 1
GROWING INTO OUR CONVICTIONS

Be ready to give an account for the hope that is in you, and do it with gentleness and reverence. (1 Peter 3:15, AP)

In ancient times, hundreds of Christians, under interrogation, refused to bow down to the empire's gods, stood their ground and declared, "I believe in God the Father almighty, maker of heaven and earth," and were executed for saying so. They had not long before left their old life behind and risked everything by choosing Christianity. In those days, new converts were instructed in the faith for months, during which time they fasted, abstained from entertainment and sex, and were prayed over diligently by the church elders. An all-night prayer vigil culminated at dawn on Easter when the converts waded out into a pool of water and were asked: "Do you believe in God the Father almighty, maker of heaven and earth? Do you believe in Jesus Christ his only Son, our Lord?" After being baptized, they were anointed with oil, dressed in a white robe, and given a drink of milk and honey, powerful symbols of their new life in Christ.

Every time we say the Apostles' Creed, we step into a long, steady river, the great two-thousand year story of believers, missionaries,

1

and martyrs. When I say "I believe in God," I become part of something bigger than myself. My faith is something in me, my reaching out, my believing; but faith is also outside myself. Faith has content. I attach myself to something old. Modern culture fawns after novelties, the latest fads. Christians look at the world with old eyes; as John Henry Newman put it, "Great acts take time." Ultimate truth cannot have been cooked up just last night, and ultimate truth does not materialize in my mind in a flash. "Deep convictions are not hazarded, but grown into slowly, obscurely and often painfully acquired" (Nicholas Lash).[1]

The Apostles' Creed helps us grow into our convictions. To believe without the Creed would be like baking without a measuring cup or building furniture without a ruler. We read the Bible, we sing hymns, we ask questions and reflect together on theology, and it is easy to miss the forest for the trees. What is at the heart of what we believe? We will use the Apostles' Creed to discover what we believe, and don't believe, to figure out who we are and how to live.

The word *credo* means "I believe." Do we live in a disbelieving age? or in an overly credulous age? We are titans of doubt and cynicism, and yet advertisers and TV shows make our heads spin over nothing at all. Faith is not believing impossible things. Faith is what I give my heart to. Faith is how I view the universe; just as Copernicus yanked our perspective so we see the world isn't flat, and the earth isn't in the center of things, so the Creed suggests there is a deeper dimension than the stage we normally stroll upon, and we aren't in the middle of things. God is.

"I believe" is not the same as saying "I feel" or "I want" or "I think," but rather, "God is"—and I fling myself upon God, I attach myself to God. Nicholas Lash wrote that, theologically, "I believe" is grammatically equivalent to "I promise": "'I believe' does not express an opinion, however well founded or firmly held, concerning God's existence. It promises that life and love, mind, heart, and all my actions, are set henceforward steadfastly on God, and God alone."[2]

The Creed is not a list of facts so much as it is an act of worship, an act of prayer. The Creed's logic teaches us how our religious ideas hang together. "Words take meaning from the company they keep" (Lash).[3] And the words take on their only valid meaning when our lives are changed. Our faith is something we do; our faith comes to life when we engage in those peculiar practices Christians count on to keep their minds and bodies in sync. It would be worse than futile to expend mental energy on the Creed while shielding our practical lives from transformation, which is our true worship.[4]

LESSON 2
DOUBT AND DOGMA

They did not understand what he was saying and were afraid to ask. (Mark 9:32, AP)

But what if we have doubts and hard questions? Does the Apostles' Creed alienate thinkers? The Creed, in a surprising way, invites doubt. The Creed was first composed as a set of questions, and for people with plenty of questions. If we know all the answers, we forget the questions! And if Jesus did anything in his ministry, he asked far more questions than he answered. Isn't there a faithfulness in our doubting? Haven't all great discoveries in history happened because somebody doubted? We have to learn to trust our questions, to think more deeply, never to quit in our pursuit of truth, to probe the pages of the Bible, to listen to the pulse of our lives, to pray more fervently. If we think cocksure certainty is the only posture for the faithful Christian, we will wind up mean or disillusioned.

The Creed does not banish doubt so much as it offers up a hopeful frame within which to ask our questions and to grow in our love for God and our heart for serving God. A vital relationship with God is not easy; the life of faith has its dark moments, as we grasp after a God who is palpable one moment and elusive the next. We shrink before a God beyond comprehension, and yet even as we shrink, we stay, not to toy with a mere idea of God, but to flourish in a startling friendship with the living God.[5]

In this series, we will explore the hard questions that dog people outside (and inside) the Church. Can anyone prove there is a God? What about science and the Bible? How can God be good if there is evil? Why call God "Father"? Does it matter if Mary was a virgin? Doctrine, we might remember, is the extravagant effort of Christian thinkers to make sense out of a faith that is complex, and one that is never embarrassed by awkward questions.

We may all know fervent Christians bristling with faith who say, "Just give me Jesus." But the Creed not only gives us Jesus. In Rowan

Williams's lovely words, it is "the job of doctrine . . . to *hold us still* before Jesus. When that slips out of view, we begin instead to use this language to defend ourselves, to denigrate others, to control and correct—and then it becomes a problem."[6]

Doctrine is holding us still before Jesus! So working through the Creed could never be dull or boring. The mystery writer Dorothy Sayers suggested that "it is the neglect of dogma that makes for dullness. The Christian faith is the most exciting drama that ever staggered the imagination of man—and the dogma *is* the drama. That drama is summarized quite clearly in the Creeds."[7] And the excitement of the drama played out in the Creed is never just a mind game; the Creed issues in a radically altered life, as we will see in each chapter of this book. Sayers, grousing about the demise of Christianity in Great Britain a half century ago, may have prophesied where we have wound up in America:

> It is worse than useless for Christians to talk about the importance of Christian morality, unless they are prepared to take their stand upon the fundamentals of Christian theology. It is fatal to let people suppose that Christianity is only a mode of feeling. . . . And it is fatal to imagine that everybody knows quite well what Christianity is and needs only a little encouragement to practice it. The brutal fact is that in this Christian country not one person in a hundred has the faintest notion what the Church teaches about God or man or society or the person of Jesus Christ.[8]

We want to be sure we at least are clear about what the Church teaches and about the true nature of morality. If we look closely into the nooks and crannies of the Creed, we will be drawn into a scintillating, changed life together.

LESSON 3
A SUMMARY OF THE BIBLE STORY

All scripture is inspired by God and is useful for teaching.
(2 Timothy 3:16, AP)

A legend circulated in the early Church: after the Spirit descended on the disciples at Pentecost, Peter said, "I believe in God the Father

Almighty." Andrew added, "and in Jesus Christ his only Son our Lord." And so they went around the table, a dozen disciples, a dozen sentences forming the Apostles' Creed. A lovely (if fabricated) legend.

Yet this impulse to trace the Creed to the living characters of the Bible is on target. "What the Scriptures say at length, the Creed says briefly" (Nicholas Lash).[9] The Apostles' Creed is a quick summary of the sixty-six books of the Bible, a bird's-eye view of the high points of the story spanning thousands of years. How easy it is to get mired in the 1,189 chapters and 31,000-plus verses of the very long Bible; the Creed helps us get our arms around the big story, or perhaps the Creed helps the story of God's mighty acts get God's arms around us.

For centuries, the Creed was especially important, for a majority of Christians did not know how to read.[10] So the Creed indelibly impressed on the eager but illiterate heart the story of God's love in this world. Perhaps in our own day, when people know how to read but often spend vast sums of time with higher tech media (or when people own Bibles that gather dust from lack of use), the Creed may be the most convenient vehicle to remind us of the one story that ultimately matters.

Notice the Creed isn't a list of dogmatic propositions. Its sentences are not like a deck of cards that could be shuffled and still be a creed. The Creed tells a story, in chronological order: God is first, then God creates; then God sends Jesus, who is born, dies, and is raised; and then the Holy Spirit dawns on the Church and its life. How fortunate we are that the Bible is a story and that the Creed is a story, for my life feels like a story. If I say, "Tell me about yourself," you don't really reveal yourself until you tell me a good story or two that unveils the depth of who you are. The Creed's words hang together with a plot; unlike a quiz in which the teacher says, "Only seven of these ten need be attempted in the allotted time," the Creed's phrases flow from one to the next.

The Creed's story flows from God to us, not vice versa. We know about God, not because we are shrewd or spiritual, but because God has lovingly, mercifully revealed God's heart to us in history. "God is the One who has made Himself known in His own revelation, and not the one man thinks out for himself and describes as God" (Karl Barth).[11]

Within the Bible itself, we discover several "creeds" used during Bible times. The ancient Israelites recited Deuteronomy 26:6-8 in worship: "The Egyptians afflicted us; we cried to the Lord; and the Lord brought us out of Egypt with a mighty hand" (AP). The early Christians recited (and probably sang) summaries of what they believed. "There is one God, and one mediator, Christ Jesus, who gave himself as a ransom" (1 Timothy 2:5-6, AP). "Christ was in the form of God, but emptied himself, born in our likeness, humbled himself, obedient unto death on a cross" (Philippians 2:6-8, AP).

Oddly enough, the best way to understand the Apostles' Creed is to dig into the Bible. If we don't know the Bible, or if we steel ourselves against the mysterious work the Bible can do in our souls, then the Creed will seem arbitrary: "We only discover the meaning of the Creed in the measure that the Bible stays an open book" (Nicholas Lash).[12]

The Bible, of course, requires interpretation. We think about it, probe, question its words, and let them question us.

> Christianity is more than a set of devotional practices and a moral code: it is also a way of thinking about God, us, the world and history. For Christians, thinking is part of believing. Augustine wrote, "No one believes anything unless one first thinks it believable. . . . Not everyone who thinks believes, since many think in order not to believe; but everyone who believes thinks" (Robert Wilken).[13]

Some who explore the Bible and Creed think in order *not* to believe! But we want to think and believe, not to believe and avoid thinking, for Jesus told us the truth would set us free. Thinking, after all, is intensely personal, as we will see in lesson 4.

LESSON 4
THE PERSONAL, SPIRITUAL QUEST

As a deer longs for flowing streams, so my soul longs for you, O God. (Psalm 42:1, AP)

Somehow in modern times, the whole idea of a creed seems arid, remote, as if some faceless bureaucrat is imposing upon free people who should think for themselves. The Apostles' Creed can become mindless, rote, pointless; and most people I talk with are eager for a direct, personal relationship with God, and aren't sure why they might benefit from a two-thousand-year-old creed. So in this last introductory lesson, let us underline how deeply personal the Creed can become. The very word "creed" originally meant "give my heart to." Evelyn Underhill noticed "how close the connection is between the great doctrines of religion and the 'inner life': how rich and splendid is the Christian account of reality, and how much food it has to offer to the contemplative soul."[14]

The Creed hints at a beautiful thought—that there is such a thing as truth, that genuine truth is not an imposition forced upon us, but rather is an open door through which we walk out into the marvelous space of life with God. We live in a culture highly suspicious of authority; but the Christian faith, luckily for us, still steps forward lovingly and teaches a story that does not diminish me or you. We find our personal fulfillment when we discover our place in the broader work of God in space and time. Otherwise we get stuck in our own egos, and our faith is nothing more than me and my private biases and preferences. "A faith which does not find its justification outside itself remains imprisoned in its own ego and cannot be sustained" (Wolfhart Pannenberg).[15] Should Christianity adjust itself to me and my spiritual quest? Or do I discover myself beyond myself? Don't I need a truth that is bigger than me, that challenges my private biases and preferences so I might grow?

Why listen to ancient authors who penned a creed centuries ago? The Church's first theologians were masters of the spiritual life, saints, martyrs, people of intense prayer who took Communion almost daily, people of immense learning who read the Scriptures deeply, passionate to the point of giving up their own lives for the truth. When they disagreed, they seized the opportunity to refine their thinking and discover an even higher truth. Nicholas Lash described their controversies as "people learning to make music, to move closer to the harmony of God, in whom alone all things hold still."[16]

One of those ancient theologians, after sitting through weeks of heated sessions debating fine points of theology, wrote this:

> The holy fathers dealt with problems by common debate. When a
> disputed question is raised in communal discussion, the light of

7

truth drives out the shadows of falsehood. The truth cannot be made clear in any other way than when there are debates about questions of faith, since everyone requires the assistance of his neighbor.[17]

I need the assistance of my neighbor to grow into my convictions. The Creed is a way for us, together, to learn to make music, and heated discussion yields more light and drives out falsehood. The Apostles' Creed began with "I believe," but soon all the other major creeds (like the Nicene Creed) shifted to "We believe." Believing is something we do together. "Personal" does not have to mean "private" or "individualistic." When I think about what is "personal" to me, I think about my relationships with other people. The Creed reminds me that I am not sawed off out on a limb when I believe. I believe with you; you believe with me; we help each other to believe; we believe for each other when it's hard to believe. We even have a mystical fellowship with Christians across the globe, and throughout the ages of history. And that is the beauty of the Creed.

So, neighbor, I invite you to this time of thinking, reflection, and even heated discussion together as we work our way through the various sentences of the Creed. I am excited, and I pray to God that through this we will grow in our relationship with God, and with one another. Thank you for joining me in this quest!

Historical Footnote

There are literally hundreds of creeds. Yale just put out a definitive publication that runs to five thick volumes (with accompanying DVD), costing $995.[18] Jaroslav Pelikan, the editor, notices "their sheer repetitiveness" and how "the differences between them must seem to any modern reader to be so minute that only a specialist would be able to tell the positions apart, or would even be interested enough to care to do so."[19] To learn more about creeds, go to www.creeds.net. If you are preaching or teaching the creeds, you would be wise to retrieve those dusty church history volumes from seminary days and relive the controversies that gave birth to the creeds.

The Apostles' Creed is ancient, although we don't know who wrote it. Originally it was used as Q&A for converts to the faith preparing for Baptism. The more official creed Christians would use was formalized in the year 325, when the emperor Constantine, himself a new convert, summoned more than two hundred bishops to meet at Nicaea (modern Iznik in Turkey) to settle some disagreements about the nature of Jesus. What does it mean to call Jesus divine? And how do we sort out the linkage of the divine and the human in Jesus? Did God make Jesus? Or was Jesus always there? If God shares divinity, is God still God? Debate was heated, but St. Athanasius and his colleagues won the day, arguing that Christ was truly God and always had been, and yet was as fully human as you and me; anything less, and our salvation would be at risk; any less and we would no longer be faithful to the stories in the Bible.

These theologians sought unity, struggling to find the language, the mental categories, to understand who Jesus was, how God works, and how we therefore understand the Christian life. Their ideas were tried, tested, retested, argued, settled upon, reargued; the net result of all this concentrated wisdom and debate was the Nicene Creed, which was revised after more bishops met in 381 at Constantinople, retooled in Ephesus in 431, touched up yet again at Chalcedon (across the Bosporus from Istanbul) in 451, each revision responding to hard questions raised within the Church, and often responding to critics outside the Church.

Millions of people scooped up copies of Dan Brown's *The Da Vinci Code* when it was first published and stumbled upon, slipped into this page-turner, an alleged exposé of early Christianity, suggesting that competing groups jockeyed for power, and that our creeds are the platform espoused by the winners who crushed (and silenced) their foes. But this is not actually how the story unfolded. One theologian did not thump the others, nor did he have a bigger sword. The theologians whose ideas emerged in the creed had the better ideas, they had the logic on their side, they had a better case given all the Bible says, and they also were more in line with the real religious practices of regular rank-and-file Christians of their day. Generally, the Christians who "won" were holy, prayerful people, most of whom had been beaten and imprisoned for their faith; some (such as St. Athanasius) could be ferocious and not always gentle with their foes, but they were theologians more than power brokers.

The fashioning of the Creed was driven by what real, down-to-earth Christians had experienced. Consider what Luke Timothy Johnson has written:

The creed does not appear suddenly in history as an imposition from on high. It has been there from the first moments . . . , from the first impulse to articulate experience, from the first effort to defend against distortion, from the first attempt to summarize the story by which this new thing in the world claimed at once to be the people of the one God, yet touched more profoundly and intimately by God than humans had ever before imagined, in the flesh of Jesus, in the Spirit of the risen Lord.[20]

In striving to understand that profound experience, the Creed helped Christians spot (and avoid) inadequate, misleading versions of Christianity that were not only unfaithful to the Bible, but also subtly dangerous to the inner spirit.

It is interesting to notice that paganism and other religions that were popular during the early years of the Church had no creeds at all. Religion for the pagans was not much about truth, and there was always room for ever more gods. Once you say, "There is one God, and there is such a thing as truth," and especially if you say that truth is embodied in this one human person, Jesus, you need to be able to declare that truth, to sort out what's true and what isn't. Throughout history, Christians have learned the creeds, rethought what the words mean, reconsidered the logic connecting our beliefs, and have published newer creeds, not to replace the older Apostles' and Nicene Creeds, but to clarify more fully for modern times their meaning and implications. Just to have a creed, then, proves that we care about truth and that truth doesn't lurk around any old corner.

Notes

1. Nicholas Lash, *Believing Three Ways in One God: A Reading of the Apostles' Creed* (Notre Dame: University of Notre Dame, 1992), 18.

2. Ibid.; see also Theodore W. Jennings, *Loyalty to God: The Apostles' Creed in Life and Liturgy* (Nashville: Abingdon Press, 1992), 14.

3. Lash, *Believing Three Ways in One God,* 14.

4. Vladimir Lossky, *The Mystical Theology of the Eastern Church* (Crestwood, N.Y.: St. Vladimir's Seminary Press, 2002), 8, demonstrates how, in the Eastern Orthodox tradition, the faithful "must live the dogma expressing a revealed truth, which appears to us as an unfathomable mystery, in such a fashion that instead of assimilating the mystery to our mode of understanding, we should, on the contrary, look

for a profound change, an inner transformation of spirit, enabling us to experience it mystically."

5. Madeleine L'Engle, *Walking on Water: Reflections on Faith and Art* (Colorado Springs: Shaw, 2001), 28, speaks of "the faithfulness of doubt," quoting Unamuno: "Those who believe they believe in God, but without passion in the heart, without anguish of mind, without uncertainty, without doubt, and even without despair, believe only in the idea of God, not in God himself."

6. Rowan Williams, *Christ on Trial: How the Gospel Unsettles Our Judgment* (Grand Rapids: Eerdmans, 2000), 37. Jaroslav Pelikan (*Credo: Historical and Theological Guide to Creeds and Confessions of Faith in the Christian Tradition* [New Haven: Yale, 2003], 65) writes, "When in the interest of the authenticity of the 'experience of Christ as my personal Savior' . . . faith is drained of its doctrinal content, neither the personal Christian experience nor its authenticity can long endure."

7. Dorothy L. Sayers, *Creed or Chaos? Why Christians Must Choose Either Dogma or Disaster* (Manchester, N.H.: Sophia Institute Press, 1995), 5.

8. Ibid., 44.

9. Lash, *Believing Three Ways in One God*, 8.

10. Frances Young, *The Making of the Creeds* (London: SCM, 1991), 4, refers to Cyril of Jerusalem, who said, "Since all cannot read the scriptures, some being hindered from knowing them by lack of education, and others by want of leisure, we comprise the whole doctrine of the Bible in a few lines."

11. Karl Barth, *Dogmatics in Outline*, trans. G. T. Thomson (New York: Harper, 1959), 23.

12. Lash, *Believing Three Ways in One God*, 9.

13. Robert Wilken, *The Spirit of Early Christian Thought: Seeking the Face of God* (New Haven: Yale, 2003), xiii.

14. Evelyn Underhill, *The School of Charity: Meditations on the Christian Creed* (Harrisburg, Pa.: Morehouse Publishing, 1991), xiii.

15. Wolfhart Pannenberg, *The Apostles' Creed in Light of Today's Questions* (Eugene: Wipf & Stock, 2000), 10.

16. Lash, *Believing Three Ways in One God*, 7.

17. Pelikan, *Credo*, 187, a comment recorded at the fifth ecumenical council at Constantinople in the sixth century.

18. Jaroslav Pelikan and Valerie Hotchkiss, eds., *Creeds and Confessions of Faith in the Christian Tradition*, 4 vols. (books and CD-rom) (New Haven: Yale, 2003).

19. Pelikan, *Credo*, 7.

20. Luke Timothy Johnson, *The Creed: What Christians Believe and Why It Matters* (New York: Doubleday, 2003), 38f.

C h a p t e r   T w o

GOD THE FATHER ALMIGHTY

LESSON 5
I BELIEVE IN GOD

I believe; help my unbelief! (Mark 9:24)

I wish I could devise the ultimate, compelling proof that God exists. Belief in God has always been hard, but we live in especially perilous times, as cynicism is in cahoots with apathy, with godlessness sprayed all over our culture. I have rational proofs in mind, but you can never compel another person mentally to believe, because belief is not merely mental. When we profess, "I believe in God," we cannot mean simply, "I think a supreme being exists," or even, "I have spiritual feelings in me." We mean something more all-embracing: we mean, "I commit myself to God."

In Old Testament times, if you asked someone on the street, "How many gods are there?" she would have answered, "Well, plenty, but we serve only one." Plenty of gods clamor for our attention, but what then do we mean by "god"? Martin Luther suggested that "whatever your heart clings to is really your god." To what do you cling? What ultimately matters to you? What motivates you? What can ruin your day? The question is: are you attached to something that is big enough to be God? or are you hooked on a mere pretender, or what in Bible times they called an "idol"?

Idols abound; John Calvin suggested that the human heart is a factory of idols. Martin Luther King, Jr. said that "there is so much frustration because we have relied on gods rather than God. We have genuflected before the god of pleasure only to discover thrills play out and are short-lived. We have bowed before the god of money only to learn there are such things as love and friendship that money can't buy."[1] The false gods in our crazed culture peddle their wares, promising us the moon, but leaving us hollow, luring us (like the sirens of mythology) into shipwreck.

In the Bible, the one true God brooks no competition; God is a "jealous" God, not because God is small-minded and petty, but because God's love for us is so immense that God cannot stand idly by while we squander ourselves on what is a mere idol, on what will only chew away at whatever is good in the soul and leave us as superficial people with pointless lives. Belief in God excludes other loyalties. To believe is to make a choice, a real-life choice, about our priorities and about where we invest our time, our energy, our money, our heart. Lash zeroed in on this issue: "Christianity is an educational project, in which we may learn, however slowly . . . some freedom from the destructive bondage which the worship of any creature, however large or powerful, beautiful or terrifying, interesting or important, brings."[2]

How might we prove God's existence? No greater proof could be advanced than the changed lives of those who say they believe in God. Many disbelieve in God precisely because they look at believers and see nothing but a mirror image of the world that cares nothing for God. "I believe in God" is subversive, countercultural, life-changing. Because of God, I am different, you are different, we are different. Perhaps the problem today is not that people cannot mentally believe in God. Perhaps, instead, they would prefer to live without God. The problem isn't a lack of belief, but an unwillingness for our lives to be changed.

But then, our resistance to change is the most self-destructive stupidity of which we are capable, for the God who pleads for our belief, for our hearts, is the God who promises us the moon, but then gives us the stars, the God who is "the Father Almighty," the subject of our next lesson.

LESSON 6
. . . THE FATHER ALMIGHTY (PART 1)

When you pray, say "Our Father." (Matthew 6:9, AP)

By definition, God must be all-mighty, and the Bible goes to great lengths to persuade us never to underestimate the omnipotence of God. "For with God nothing will be impossible" (Luke 1:37). Yet, omnipotence can feel impersonal, maybe even intimidating; before raw power, we cower. "Omnipotence can be feared, but never loved" (Jürgen Moltmann).[3] God could not bear to be known as merely "Almighty," so God decided, "I will be their Father." We believe in God "the Father Almighty."

Of course, many modern people question how a good God could be all-mighty, with all the agonized suffering that goes on. We will not dodge these questions, but we will need to wait until chapters 6 through 8 to think through where exactly God turns up in the face of suffering.

Many modern people question calling God "Father." Some fathers are distant, cold, or harsh, and children who grow up with such fathers can be terribly confused about God. Some people ask why we use "Father" instead of "Mother." We know God is not a male, and men frequently do not behave in Godlike ways. The Bible itself is adorned with feminine images for God; and I love these words from the medieval mystic, Julian of Norwich:

> As truly as God is our Father, so truly is God our Mother, and he reveals this in everything, saying to us, "I am the power and goodness of fatherhood; I am the wisdom and the tender love of motherhood; I am the light and the grace which is all blessed love; I am the great supreme goodness of every thing; I make you to love; I cause you to long; I am the fulfillment of all your desires."[4]

We call God "Father" for one reason only: when Jesus spoke to God, he called God "Abba," an Aramaic word that a little child would use when curled up on the father's lap; even a grown child would continue to use this endearing term of affection. Jesus enjoyed such an intimate relationship with the "almighty" God that he spoke to him tenderly as "Abba." The disciples noticed and marveled. Jesus' whole mission, we might say, was to invite them (and us) to discover what it is to curl up on the lap of almighty God, look up, and simply say, "Abba."

Jesus taught us to pray "Our Father." This intimacy seems presumptuous; how dare we? For we are so different from God, so distant, so un-dependent, so frivolous and naughty at times. Jesus grants us an astounding permission: you, even you, can be on such intimate terms with the holy God. This is all grace, of course. When an infant is baptized, we witness the humbling, hopeful truth that we are small, vulnerable, entirely dependent on the unearnable mercy of God, and we remain forever that way. We always live before God as those who are, as Karl Barth phrased it, "inept, inexperienced, unskilled, and immature. [We] may and can be masters and even virtuosos in many things, but never in what makes [us] Christians, God's children."[5] Jesus said, "Unless you turn and become like children, you will never enter the kingdom of heaven" (Matthew 18:3). Notice also Jesus taught us to pray "Our Father" (instead of "My Father")! We do not believe alone; we need not go solo, and in fact, we cannot. We are saved to be part of a community, part of a family: the body of Christ. And we may even pray on behalf of those who do not pray and acknowledge for even them that God is *our* Father.

We may also recall that in the biblical world, sons were apprenticed to their fathers; they learned their trade from watching and mimicking the fathers. So, "saying 'our father' isn't just the boldness of walking into the presence of the living and almighty God and saying, 'Hi, Dad.' It is the boldness of saying 'Please may I, too, be considered an apprentice son.' It means signing on for the kingdom of God" (Tom Wright).[6]

LESSON 7
. . . THE FATHER ALMIGHTY (PART 2)

His father saw him, and was filled with compassion. (Luke 15:20, AP)

Two famous paintings can help us probe deeply into the Creed's first sentence. The Hermitage in St. Petersburg houses Rembrandt's final effort (among many) to capture the return of the prodigal son on canvas. Rembrandt knew personally the acute agony of loss, having lived long enough to see three sons, two daughters, and his wife die. Henri Nouwen wrote a lovely devotional reflection *(The Return of the Prodigal Son: A Story of Homecoming)* on this painting, asking, "Had I really ever dared to step into the center, kneel down, and let myself be held by a forgiving God?" instead of "choosing over and over again the position of the outsider looking in." In the world, we strive feverishly for meaning, ignorant of God's firm, tender embrace. Studying the hands Rembrandt painted of the father holding his son come home, Nouwen wrote,

> In them mercy becomes flesh; upon them forgiveness and healing come together. . . . I felt drawn to those hands; I have come to know those hands. They have held me from the hour of my conception, they welcomed me at birth, they held me close to my mother's breast, fed me, kept me warm. They have protected me in times of danger, they have waved me goodbye and always welcomed me back. Those hands are God's hands. . . . They are also the hands of my parents, teachers, friends, all God has given me to remind me how safely I am held.[7]

Nothing sexist here, as Nouwen observes how the hands are painted differently. "The father's left hand touching the son's shoulder is strong and muscular. I see a certain pressure, especially in the thumb. That hand seems not only to touch, but, with its strength, also to hold. How different is the father's right hand! This hand does not hold or grasp. It is refined, soft, and very tender. It wants to caress, to stroke, and to offer consolation and comfort. It is a mother's hand. The Father is not simply a great patriarch. He is mother as well as father. He holds, and she caresses. He confirms and she consoles." Rembrandt was near death when he painted this in 1668, and as it turns out, Nouwen himself died in 1996 while working on a documentary film about this painting.

Around the year 1300, Giotto devised a series of frescoes that narrate pictorially the life of St. Francis. In the third bay of the upper basilica of the cathedral in Assisi, we see the dramatic moment when Francis, being sued by his father Pietro Bernardone, abandoned his worldly goods, and even all ties with his father. His nakedness shielded by the cloak of the Bishop Guido, Francis lifts a hand toward heaven, where God's hand of blessing gestures toward him. It was at this moment that Francis solemnly announced, "Pietro Bernardone is no longer my father; my father from now on is 'Our Father, who art in heaven.'" For Francis, to call God "Father" was a declaration of allegiance, choosing to serve God even if it elicited his earthly father's wrath. Perhaps we may be pressed to make a similar choice, remembering what Jesus said: "If anyone comes to me and does not hate his own father . . . he cannot be my disciple" (Luke 14:26). To call God "Father" is not all warm and fuzzy, but exacts a radical obedience from us.

A DEEPER REFLECTION
I Wish My Father Had Done That

To plunge into the Apostles' Creed may seem as foolish as jumping into an old cement pool that hasn't held water for years. People say to me, "I've got to figure out my faith for myself. Nobody else can tell me what and how to believe." And we do need to figure it out for ourselves. But I don't know about you: if somebody says to me, "James, you've got to figure out your faith for yourself," I begin to feel lonely, boxed in. Even though I had the privilege of studying and earning degrees in theology, I have no wish to be a soloist; I prefer joining the choir. If I think of myself as a solitary mountain climber on my way toward God, I'm not sure I would risk the journey: who will catch me when I make a mistake? The odds that my thoughts about God happen to be the ultimate truth for all reality are embarrassingly small. We need one another. We need ancestors, friends from distant lands, saints of old, little children. The image for believing is not the solitary mountain climber, but rather friends and family sitting around a table breaking bread, having extended after-dinner conversation together. We help one another believe. We help one another grow into our faith. We help one another correct those places where we have misunderstandings of God. We help one another believe when it is hard for us to believe.

18

I want to believe in something that is bigger than me and my thoughts about God. Sometimes I talk to people who don't believe in God, or those who are not sure they believe in God. They *do* have awfully good questions, and however valiantly I may try to resolve them, my regiment of pro-God arguments can never decisively win the day. Yes, we use our brains, we rally our ideas, firm in a faith that is far from irrational, proud of a faith that thrives on intellectual rigor. But at the end of the day, the only compelling case to be made for God would be the dramatically changed lives of those who believe in God. Exhibits A, B, and C as proofs for God would be the lawyer abandoning his career to serve the poorest who have no other advocate, the stone-cold marriage revived, the woman divulging remarkable traces of joy in the face of adversity. The only logic on which we might rely is deeply personal. To say "I believe in God" is never reduced to "I believe that there *is* a God." Instead, the grammar is equivalent to what I did at the altar on March 1, 1986, when I looked at Lisa and made promises to her. "I promise that I will love you in sickness and in health, forsaking all others, 'til death do us part." This is what we mean when we say "I believe in God, the Father Almighty."

Power and Love

If belief is about love, if a "god" is what we give our heart to, then we may be puzzled by the Creed's seemingly incompatible pair, "Father" and "Almighty." How could a God who is all-mighty also be like a Father, and vice versa? I am in the middle of taking a stab at being a father myself; and although I cannot remember the rosy scenario I presumed parenting would be before I got into it, I am certain I assumed I was going to be more almighty than I am. If there is anything a father is *not* nowadays, it is "almighty."

How shall we say it? God is almighty. We know that God is almighty, but God can't bear to be known only as almighty. Because, were a father or any person to be truly almighty, it would scare the daylights out of everyone, and especially the children. Almighty is intimidating, squashing, fearsome. Before almightiness, we shiver. So how can you love someone who is all-powerful? Perhaps this is why fathers aren't all mighty—because if you're almighty, a despot in your household, then you can't be loved, and fathers want so very much to be loved. Isn't this why God says, "I shall be not just almighty, but I shall be your father"? When Jesus prayed, he did not call God "Almighty." Instead he spoke to God as "Abba," the Aramaic word Jesus beautifully spoke as one of his very first words—not his first words in his teaching ministry, but his first words as an infant groping after the wonder of speech. Jesus, held lovingly in Joseph's arms, looked up into his eyes and called him "Abba," delighting Mary's husband. As a grown man, Jesus had that kind of intimate, tender relationship with Almighty God. The disciples got a glimpse of the grown man Jesus as a little child, sitting on God's lap, looking up tenderly and calling on his Abba. The disciples envied this of him, and they wanted in on it. They said, "We want to have that kind of relationship with God."

The Elusive Father

But wasn't Jesus just as intimate (or more intimate) with Mary, his mother? How much do we really want to invest in the very opening of the Creed, "I believe in God the Father"? We wonder about using a gender image for God that excludes half of humanity—or worse, one that includes half that isn't so godlike. I see this in counseling all the time: people harbor confusion about God, and a lot of it is because they do believe that God is like their own father. You see, if you had a father who is cold or distant, harsh or sophomoric, then you get confused about what God ought to be. If God is like that kind of father, then I don't want to have anything to do with him, or we stumble into a dysfunctional faith. I want to plead that God is the best father imaginable, but aren't our imaginations on this subject a little clouded?

I thought all this past week about being a father myself. When I am a guest speaker, the hosts request a résumé so I can be properly introduced. I really do mean it when I say the only thing worth mentioning is that I have the privilege of being father to these three children. I am continually surprised by how much I love my children. But I can't get too maudlin about it, for I am also continually surprised by how frustrating and numbingly exasperating being a father can be. I have been dizzied by unanticipated delights, and my heart has been broken in places I didn't know were there. Question: is it like that for God? If God is our Father, our "Abba," does God look down at us and at one moment it's an unexpected delight, and then the next moment God's heart is broken? The prophet Hosea speaks directly out of God's heart: "I have been a father to them, I love them, but the more I love, the more they run from me, they bolt away and I can't decide whether to rage with anger or hang my head and weep" (11:9, paraphrase). Is it like that for God?

Closeness. I want to be close to my children, and they to me. But how shall I say it? Even if you have lucked into the best relationship imaginable with your father, or if as a father you have cultivated the best imaginable relationship with your children, the truth is there's some dysfunction in the heart of that, there's some mystery. You may think you know your father thoroughly, but then you look at him and his life again, and there's something profoundly important you'd totally missed, something you flat-out can never comprehend. Indeed, the saddest stories I hear are from parents and children who cannot decipher meaningful connections between what the other one says, does, and means. Norman McLean, in *A River Runs Through It*, says, "It is those we live with and love and should know who elude us."[8] We live with God, God lives with us; we should know each other. Yet God eludes us; we elude God. Did Jesus let the disciples overhear him praying intimately to God as "Abba" so they might get themselves prepared, so we might not throw up our hands in despair when life with God really does mirror life with the dads we have known, loved, wounded, missed, misunderstood, been wounded by, and even lost?

Somewhere over the Rainbow

When my daughter Sarah was just four years old, she went on stage for the very first time to sing in our church talent show. Cabaret style, I perched her on the piano with a candelabra next to her, and I played as she sang "Somewhere over the Rainbow." I can tell you without any bias at all that Judy Garland never sang it so beautifully. The song ended, my church members erupted into a standing ovation (what else do you do for the preacher's daughter?), we took a few bows, and then we walked offstage where no one could see but us except a single crew person, one of my most stalwart church workers. I hoisted Sarah up in my arms, twirled her 360 degrees, kissed her and said "Sarah, I love you so much." Two feet away, the crew person looked at me with eyes I cannot quite describe and said, "I wish my father had done that." A little slow on the uptake, I asked, "You wish your father had played the piano?" With a choked pain in her sixty-year-old voice, she said, "No. I wish my father had loved me."

I don't know if her father loved her or not, but what I do know is that there is some ache at the heart of our lives. There is some place where a father is supposed to be, and I wonder if God didn't anticipate the darkness of that place and decided, "I will be known as father to my children, because I cannot bear for them to struggle with no hope. I will be Father, however dimly grasped, by those who have pretty good fathers, by those who struggle with fathers among the quick and the dead." People have politicized and militarized the term *9/11* as a code, but every time I hear *9/11,* I think about children I don't know personally in some apartment in Manhattan or in a bungalow out in Connecticut. It's been three years now, and they go to bed at night where a father used to live down the hall, but now there is no father down the hall, because he went to work for them one day, on 9/11. The politicians and pundits wax with no eloquence at all about 9/11, but for this boy, for this girl, daddy isn't there. They cannot look up at anyone and say "Daddy." "Abba." God knew this. God is always our father.

When Frederick Buechner was five years old, he heard shouts and screams outside his house. He ran down the stairs and saw his father lying in the driveway, people frantically working over his body. Suicide. A couple of days later they found a note his father had left, stuck in the last page of *Gone with the Wind.* To young Frederick and his mother the note said, "I adore you and love you, but I am no good. Give Freddie my watch. I give you all my love." Thinking back to this unspeakably horrible moment, Buechner quoted Mark Twain: "Losing somebody like that is like a house burning down. It's years before you know the extent of your loss." Buechner suggested that his father really died of heart trouble.[9]

How shall I say it? God is never gone with the wind. God is our father when we have heart trouble. We see the Father Almighty most clearly in the best story ever told by the Son who knew him best. A man loved his son more than his own life, but the son preferred to be self-made, to indulge in pleasures far from home. So the son bolted, and broke his father's heart. But one day the boy decided, "I won't put up with this two-bit life for one more day. I'm going home to my father." He comes home, not to a father who does what human fathers do (heatedly demanding, "Where have you been? How much did you waste? You'd better apologize and repay every cent!"). This was not the Abba Jesus knew. Instead, and so very fortunately for me and for you, this father sees the son coming. He's been waiting, looking, longing every day forever. He runs. Before the boy hardly gets a word out, the father scoops up that boy and twirls him around, hugs him, kisses him, weeps on his shoulder, and says, "I have missed you so much. I love you so much. Welcome home. Let the party begin" (Luke 15:11-32, AP). This is the truth of our lives. This is our hope. This is the God who is so almighty he bends down to us and whispers in our ear, "Please, call me 'Abba.'" We believe in God the Father Almighty.

Notes

1. From "Strength to Love," in *A Testament of Hope: The Essential Writings and Speeches of Martin Luther King, Jr.,* ed. James Washington (San Francisco: Harper & Row, 1986), 508.

2. Nicholas Lash, *Believing Three Ways in One God: A Reading of the Apostles' Creed* (Notre Dame: University of Notre Dame Press, 1992), 21.

3. Jürgen Moltmann, *The Crucified God,* trans. R. A. Wilson and John Bowden (Minneapolis: Fortress Press, 1993), 223.

4. Julian of Norwich, *Revelations of Divine Love,* trans. M. L. del Mastro (Garden City, N.Y.: Image Books, 1977), 59.

5. Karl Barth, *The Christian Life,* trans. Geoffrey W. Bromiley (Grand Rapids: Eerdmans, 1981), 79.

6. N. T. Wright, *The Lord and His Prayer* (Grand Rapids: Eerdmans, 1996), 19f.

7. Henri Nouwen, *The Return of the Prodigal Son: A Story of Homecoming* (New York: Doubleday, 1992), 12, 96-99.

8. Norman Maclean, *A River Runs Through It and Other Stories* (New York: Pocket, 1976), 113.

9. Frederick Buechner, *The Sacred Journey* (San Francisco: HarperSanFrancisco, 1982), 39-41.

Chapter   Three

MAKER OF HEAVEN AND EARTH

LESSON 8

MAKER OF HEAVEN AND EARTH (PART 1)

In the beginning God created the heavens and the earth.
(Genesis 1:1)

Gregory of Nyssa called the universe "a marvelously composed hymn to the power of the Almighty."[1] Saint Thomas Aquinas wrote, "In God's hand were the ends of the world: when his hand was opened by the key of love, creatures came forth."[2] Dante spoke of "the love that moves the stars."[3] The almighty God who is all love expressed that love by creating the universe, the earth, me sitting here writing, you sitting there reading, and this is our good fortune.

How God did it is best understood by the scientists. The Church has had an embarrassing relationship with science. Galileo is only the most famous of so many scientists we revere who were upbraided by Church authorities. Southern religious leaders cheered when a Tennessee court ruled to censure a teacher of evolution named Scopes. Too often, theology has fled science, fearing that science would pull the curtain back on God, as Toto did to the Wizard in Oz. Charles Darwin, having considered becoming a clergyman, boarded the *HMS Beagle* with a copy of *Paradise Lost*, and it was his faith that was lost: "I am like a man who has become colour-blind; disbelief crept over me at a very slow rate."[4]

But science, instead of shredding our faith, might actually expand our faith. When the physicist tells me the pinhole of light I see in the sky has been streaming toward me for thousands of years, when the biologist explains to me the echolocation of the bat or the visual prowess of the eagle, I finally understand that the God I've wanted to tuck in my back pocket is too small. The true God is bigger, older, more powerful, more marvelous than my mind can ever comprehend. Theodore Jennings wisely described our passion for science:

> Both science and faith stand in service to humanity, to liberate humanity and the earth itself from bondage to powers of destruction. . . . When faith seeks to hold the mind and heart captive to a particular world view, science rightly chastens faith by fulfilling its own commission to liberate from illusion and fear. Yet science, too, is capable of forgetting or misunderstanding this commission. When science becomes mere technology in the quest for power it becomes an instrument of destruction.[5]

Must we believe the world was created literally in merely six days (as in Genesis 1)? Of course not. Galileo wrote to his friend Castelli: "I believe the intention of the Holy Bible is to persuade us toward salvation, something science could never do; only the Holy Spirit can move us. But I do not think we must believe that the same God who gave us our intellect would have us put it aside and not use it."[6] God gave us brains, and God must be more delighted than anybody when we leap forward to greater knowledge of God's world.

Genesis 1 is not a physics lesson, and it was written before science had awakened in the mind of humanity. Genesis 1 is a bold proclamation of Who is the author of the universe, the force that makes it all happen, nurturing the astonishing explosion of life on this planet and the artistry of light in the farthest reaches of space. The world is not here by chance. The universe has a purpose.

LESSON 9

MAKER OF HEAVEN AND EARTH
(PART 2)

When I look at your heavens, what is man that you are mindful of him? Yet you crown him with glory and honor; you have given him dominion over the works of your hands. (Psalm 8:3-6, AP)

To contemplate God as "Maker of heaven and earth" draws me out of myself and elicits a song, a sigh, a shout of praise. "Praise the Lord!" is the Bible's ringing invitation to us to be dumbfounded before the greatness of God. I think of God: my eyes fly open; I stop and notice the works of God all around me and inside me.

Praise is cheap nowadays; ads praise everything from soap to automobiles, mindless celebrities and the latest "American idol." But the only object ultimately worthy of our adoration is God. Instead of calculating how I might use God to get what I'm after, I simply praise God. Praise is amazed by God, thunderstruck by the power and tenderness at the heart of everything. Praise is not efficient, not productive of anything except a relationship with the Maker of the universe. Charles Wesley sang of being "lost in wonder, love and praise." His brother John, with his last dying breath, sang: "I'll praise my Maker while I have breath; and when my soul is lost in death, praise shall employ my nobler powers. My days of praise shall never be past."[7]

Praise is the cure for despair, as we dare not wind up like one of Pat Conroy's characters, whose "greatest fear was that he would be buried alive in that American topsoil of despair and senselessness where one felt nothing, where being alive was simply a provable fact instead of a ticket to a magic show."[8] God's fantastically creative hand has strewn wonders all around this theater in which we find ourselves—and the least we can do is notice. Before God's magic we are reduced to slack-jawed wonder. We stop and smell the rose because the color and scent give glory to God. We shut off the lights and stare at the night sky. Christians pay attention; they notice, marvel, and give thanks.

If God is the Maker of heaven and earth, and of you and me, then my life is not my own. I depend upon God for every breath I take, for having a brain, energy, talent; it all belongs to God, and so my wishes do not count for much anymore. All that matters is what God wants me to do with my life that is really God's life, with my ability that is really God's, with my money that also is God's. My life is no longer self-indulgent, but I enjoy the privilege of serving the Maker of it all. If we believe God is the Maker and true owner, then it becomes our privilege to loosen our grip on whatever we have, and discover that our only real joy comes in what we pass along. If the whole world belongs to God, then we are a single family on this earth. Human divisions flutter away in the cool breeze of God's breath.

And if God is truly the Maker of heaven and earth, then we never lose hope. If I am made by God, then sticks and stones may break my bones, but I belong to God, and God has the power to bring me through any trial or suffering to God's good end for me. God's love is so voluminous, so touchingly personal, so unquenchable, that God made heaven—and our true citizenship rests in that future kingdom, not here on earth. Our destiny is with God, in heaven, and that heaven will make even the glorious wonders of this world pale by comparison.

A DEEPER REFLECTION
The Love That Moves the Stars

A century ago, the great orator James Weldon Johnson thought about the creation of the world, and gave us a fascinating vision:

> God sat down on the side of a hill where he could think. God thought and he thought until he thought, "I'll make me a man." Up from the bed of the river God scooped the clay, and by the bank of the river God kneeled him down and there the great God Almighty who lit the sun and fixed it in the sky, who flung the stars to the most far corner of the night, who rounded the earth in the middle of his hand, this great God like a mammy bending over her

baby kneeled down in the dust, toiling over a lump of clay till he shaped it in his own image. Then into it he blew the breath of life and the man became a living soul.[9]

God Almighty, "like a mammy bending over her baby." *How* did God, this great mammy, bend over her baby? Can't we turn to the scientists for help?

Science and Faith

Through history, the Church has more often turned *against* the scientists to clamp down on them. Ecclesiastical officials were not very charitable toward the brilliant (and faithful) Galileo. Summoned before an inquisitorial board who insisted he recant his finding that the earth is not the center of the universe, that the earth in fact moves around the sun, he bowed before Church authorities, declaring the earth stands still—only to exit the room, legendarily muttering under his breath, "But it really does move." In the Scopes "monkey trial" in 1925, William Jennings Bryan boasted that he was "more interested in the Rock of ages than in the age of rocks." Church folk hollered "Amen," but rocks really do have considerable age on them. And the grander that age, the more God is glorified. God is old, older than the most ancient rocks; God was around long before the galaxies began casting light our way a hundred thousand years ago. Planet earth, thankfully, is *not* the center of the universe; the center is occupied by God.

The scientific revolution may feel scary to faith. "The Darwinian revolution knocked out the back wall, revealing eerie lighted landscapes as far back as we can see. Almost at once, Albert Einstein and astronomers with reflector telescopes and radio telescopes knocked out the other walls and the ceiling, leaving us sunlit exposed, and drifting" (as Annie Dillard put it).[10] But maybe if the walls are knocked down and we drift a ways, we will see further, more deeply, and sense our need to be held. Jesus did say, "You shall know the truth and the truth shall set you free." Science need not put us on a path contrary to faith. For me, the discoveries of science boggle my mind, and God is not diminished; instead I realize how small is the box into which I have tried to cram the God of immeasurable grandeur, might, and wisdom.

Tangling with a cynical, atheistic scientist has its pleasures, but arguments grind into stalemates. When a physicist like Stephen Hawking asks, "Why does the universe go to all the bother of existing?"[11] I feel I have a decent (if modest) answer. I find the richest meaning in the incontestable fact that, were the charge on an electron, or the force of gravity, different by just one-hundredth of one percent, human life could not exist. I know an evolutionist like Stephen Jay Gould will scoff and reply that this "permits no conclusion about our origin" and is "ludicrous." Yet I still feel more secure, as if there may be some purpose to me being me. I have a longtime friend, a retired professor of astronomy. When some phenomenon is about to appear in the night sky, he'll call me: "There's a meteor shower," or, "Come see the rings of Saturn and three of its moons." These wonders typically happen at 3:00 in the morning, and during the wintry months. As he completes his duties as docent in the museum of space, he often looks at me and says, "This makes me feel at home in the universe."

God's Dazzling Surprises

For my friend it is the predictability of the phenomena. Predictability, the divine ordering of the cosmos, frees us to believe that God is predictable, that God is constant, reliable. The ancients feared the machinations of the stars, leaving them cowering in superstition. But God holds the stars, the planets, and galaxies, not to mention the molecules, electrons, and positrons, in a loving, decisive hand. God is not random or arbitrary. God is good, God is constant. And yet God is full of surprises. Wolfhart Pannenberg suggested that the theory of evolution, far from shoving God out of the picture, "has given theology an opportunity to see God's ongoing creative activity not merely in the preservation of a fixed order but in the constant bringing forth of things that are new."[12] More playfully, Annie Dillard can serve as our guide in the zoo of God's profligate creation:

> Look at the horsehair worm, a yard long and thin as a thread, whipping through the duck pond. . . . Look at a turtle under ice breathing through its pumping cloaca. Look at the fruit of the osage orange tree, big as a grapefruit, green, convoluted as any human brain. Look, in short, at practically anything—the coot's

30

feet, the mantis's face, a banana, the human ear—and see that not only did the creator create everything, but that he is apt to create *anything*. He'll stop at nothing. There is no one standing over evolution with a blue pencil to say "Now that one, there, is absolutely ridiculous, and I won't have it."[13]

Look in the mirror. Walk outside, off the pavement. Shoot the street light out with a BB gun, lie down on the ground, and look straight up into the dark, which isn't dark at all. Genesis 1 is not a physics lesson. Rather, it is a sermon; it is a ballad; it is an opera with booming voices, striking costumes, laughter, and a few tears. It is a bold proclamation of who is the author of the universe, that the world is not here by chance, that God is powerful enough to hurl the stars across billions of light years and delicate enough to mix hues in the petal of a rose. If we would just look, we would see in our world the "theater of the glory of God."[14] If we would just listen, we would overhear "creation as a divine composition, a magnificent music, whose measures and refrains rise up to the pleasure and the glory of God" (David Bentley Hart).[15]

God scattered those stars in the night sky, knowing the psalmist would cry out, "What is man that you are mindful of him? Yet you have made him just a little lower than the divine" (Psalm 8:4-5, AP). God made wheat to grow in fields, grapes in vineyards, so they might be gathered and processed, so we might gather around the Lord's table and ourselves be processed into the kinds of people who notice God's work and want to get in on the action. God made donkeys, so people could travel from places like Nazareth to Bethlehem. God made mothers' wombs, the intricacies of DNA, microscopic blueprints of life, a bulb gathering momentum in the darkness, setting up a temporary shelter, pressing against mommy's tummy, then convulsing, paining her, finally exiting into the light, gulping for air, so a mother like Mary might bear her little boy and name him Jesus.

The Name of God on It

Coleridge once wrote that the Jews

would not willingly tread upon the smallest piece of paper in their way, but picked it up; for possibly, said they, the name of God may be upon it. Though there was a little superstition in this, yet truly there is nothing but good religion in it, if we apply it to man. Trample not on any; there may be some work of grace there, that thou knowest not of. The name of God may be written upon that soul thou treadest on; it may be a soul that Christ thought so much of as to give his precious blood for it; therefore despise it not.[16]

May there be some work of grace there? There is some work of grace there, and everywhere. Twice recently I was tagged as a "liberal." On the first occasion, this gentleman had read a column my daughter wrote in the newspaper, with a pro-environmentalist slant on a local issue. He asked what I thought and I said, "I'm with her." He said "Hmmph, the environment. That's liberal." This made my head hurt. Aren't you tired of these tags, these dismissive labels? With regard to the environment, if God created the world, aren't we as God's people under some obligation to care about the world that God has placed us in? Isn't it the case that every time we pave over some species that we are silencing some voice of praise that God has created in the great chorus of praise and creation?[17] Aren't we called as God's people not to look at the world as something to be used for our benefit, but to be dumbfounded, wide-eyed, lost in wonder, love, and praise? We look at the minutiae of the world; we look at the massive landscape that we find before us, and we are moved to praise God. If "liberal" means we want to remember how to be astonished and moved by the glory of God, and to nurture what God has gingerly placed into our hands, then I suppose I will be liberal—although shouldn't the effort to "conserve" God's world be dubbed "conservative"?

My second "liberal" accusation: last week after buying gas I saw a familiar face. Noticing I was in a hurry, he asked, "Where are you going?" I said, "Well, it's January 15. This is Martin Luther King, Jr.'s birthday, and every year the city of Charlotte has a service down in Marshall Park by the statue of King, and I'm the speaker." I wish I were kidding, but when I invited him to go with me, he said, "I'm not into that liberal agenda." I was for a moment sorely tempted to violate King's nonviolent principles, even if only verbally. If God is Maker of heaven and earth, then can we be anything but passionate about King's vision, which was God's vision before it was King's— dreaming of the day when little white boys and girls sit down to the table of brotherhood with little black boys and girls? Is that liberal, or is it the only logical conclusion to our belief that God is Maker of heaven and earth?

He's Got the Whole World in His Hands

Doesn't this mean that, as Christians, we can't just care about our beloved United States of America? Sometimes when pious people talk, you'd think that God lives within the confines of these fifty states and that we are the people that God wants to help, and the rest of the world can fall into a trash basket somewhere. There was an earthquake in Iran not long ago. Did you notice? If something happens in America and five people die, we're so distraught. In Iran there was an earthquake with forty to fifty thousand casualties. It was on the front page of the newspaper for one day. The second day it slipped to page 11A, and on the third day there was no news at all. Iran has not fallen off God's radar screen. God cares. If we, as the people of God, believe that God created the world, we are called to care for the entire world.

Whatever happens to you and me in this life, no matter what misfortune may befall us, we can and must say with bold hope, "Hey, I'm somebody God made. You shouldn't step on me, for God's name is written here; and I won't step on you, for God's name is written on you, too." We owe every breath to God. You can no longer glance at your watch and say, "I'm going to go out and do what I want with my time." You have to ask God, "God, what do you want me to do with the time that you've given me?" If God has given you some energy, some ability, some money, it all belongs to God. You and I have to try our best.

Paul Farmer, after his undergraduate days at Duke, went to Harvard Medical School and graduated at the top of his class. He was so brilliant that they invited him onto the Harvard faculty. But he only gives them half of each year. The other half he spends in Haiti, in the most rural, poverty-stricken section of Haiti, where people live in squalor. Paul leaves his comfortable nest in Cambridge and becomes a torch of hope for Haitians, helping them get medicine and healthcare. His accomplishments are legion; his selflessness has prompted friends to rethink what we mean by "doing your best." Or as Tracy Kidder asked, "How does one person with great talents come to exert a force on the world? I think in Farmer's case the answer lies somewhere in the apparent craziness, the sheer impracticality, of half of everything he does."[18]

When Haitians talk about God, sometimes they ask, "Why does God allow such misery?" They respond with a proverb: *Bondye konn bay, men li pa konn separe,* which is translated, "God gives, but God doesn't share." Farmer explains the adage: "God gives us humans everything we need to flourish, but he's not the one who's supposed to divvy up the loot."[19] God made me, you, them—and the loot. We want to do our very best, and if God is Maker of heaven and earth, we really have no choice but to get busy divvying up the loot.

When receiving the Nobel Peace Prize, Martin Luther King, Jr. said, "I refuse to accept the fact that the 'isness' of man's present nature makes him incapable of reaching up for the eternal 'oughtness' that forever confronts him."[20] Because God is Maker of heaven and earth, we can never give up on the eternal oughtness. God calls us to an "ought" that is higher than what "is," and the "oughtness" depends not on us, but on the power of God. If we would stop carrying the world on our shoulders, and trust in the power of God, the world could be transformed. Our community could be a far deeper, richer place. Our lives would not seem so hollow and random. We would be in sync with the God who created the universe.

The Last Thing

One last thing (or, I should say, *the* last thing): God is the maker of *heaven* and earth. We could just say God is the maker of the earth; but mercifully, God did not just make the earth and stop. God also made the heaven. Earth is a wonderful place, but this earth is not all there is. God in his mercy also made the heavens; so whatever happens on this earth, we have a home, a destination, as declared so thrillingly in the last stanza of "How Great Thou Art": "When Christ shall come with shouts of acclamation and take me home, what joy shall fill my heart!" Think, right now, of someone in your heart, someone who has died, someone who is no longer on God's good earth. If God had just made the earth, there would be nothing left for you to do but wallow in your grief. But because God made the heaven and the earth, then you can trust that that person whom you love, whom you miss, is with God, is home with the Maker of heaven and earth.

And in that heaven, little black boys and girls will hold hands with little white boys and girls. Haitians will be healthy. Liberals and conservatives will dance among the lush, green trees. The stars in their courses. Even the scientists will shout, "It really does move," the love that moves the stars.

Notes

1. Quoted in Vladimir Lossky, *The Mystical Theology of the Eastern Church* (Crestwood, N.Y.: St. Vladimir's Seminary Press, 2002), 95.
2. See Robert Jenson, *Systematic Theology,* vol. 2 (New York: Oxford University Press, 1999), 14.
3. The very last line of *The Divine Comedy: Paradise* xxxiii.145.
4. See the interesting analysis of Robert Wright, *The Moral Animal: Evolutionary Psychology and Everyday Life* (New York: Vintage, 1994), 364.
5. Theodore Jennings, *Loyalty to God: The Apostles' Creed in Life and Liturgy* (Nashville: Abingdon Press, 1992), 59.
6. Set in an intriguing context by Dava Sobel, *Galileo's Daughter: A Historical Memoir of Science, Faith and Love* (New York: Penguin, 2000), 65.
7. Stanley Ayling, *John Wesley* (Nashville: Abingdon Press, 1979), 315. The hymn he sang is by Isaac Watts.
8. Pat Conroy, *Beach Music* (New York: Doubleday, 1995), 291. For a wise reflection on praise as "the antidote to despair," see David Ford and Daniel Hardy, *Praising and Knowing God* (Louisville: Westminster, 1985).
9. James Weldon Johnson, *God's Trombones: Seven Negro Sermons in Verse* (New York: Penguin, 1976), 17-20.
10. Annie Dillard, *Teaching a Stone to Talk: Expeditions and Encounters* (New York: HarperCollins, 1982), 121.
11. Stephen W. Hawking, *A Brief History of Time: From the Big Bang to Black Holes* (London: Bantam, 1988), 174.
12. Wolfhart Pannenberg, *Systematic Theology,* vol. 2, trans. Geoffrey W. Bromiley (Grand Rapids: Eerdmans, 1994), 119.
13. Annie Dillard, *Pilgrim at Tinker Creek* (New York: Harper & Row, 1974), 135.
14. John Calvin, *Institutes* I.xiv.20; for him, God has "wonderfully adorned heaven and earth with the utmost possible abundance, variety, and beauty, like a large and splendid mansion, most exquisitely and copiously furnished."
15. David Bentley Hart, *The Beauty of the Infinite: The Aesthetics of Christian Truth* (Grand Rapids: Eerdmans, 2003), 275.
16. Discussed beautifully in *Walking on Water: Reflections on Faith and Art,* by Madeleine L'Engle (Colorado Springs: Shaw, 2001), 125.
17. Thomas Berry, *The Dream of the Earth* (San Francisco: Sierra Club, 1988), 46.
18. Tracy Kidder, *Mountains Beyond Mountains: The Quest of Dr. Paul Farmer* (New York: Random House, 2003), 8, 296.
19. Ibid., 79.
20. James Washington, ed., *A Testament of Hope: The Essential Writings and Speeches of Martin Luther King, Jr.* (San Francisco: HarperSanFrancisco, 1986), 225.

Chapter Four

JESUS CHRIST, HIS ONLY SON, OUR LORD

LESSON 10
. . . AND IN JESUS CHRIST (PART 1)

God so loved the world that he gave his only Son, that whoever
believes in him should not perish but have eternal life.
(John 3:16)

John 3:16, perhaps the most memorized Bible verse in history, is like a zoom lens, focusing us on the turning point, the fulcrum, the axis of the universe: Jesus, the subject of every kind of debate, misconstrued by millions, the hope of the ages. Nothing reveals so much about ourselves as what we make of Jesus; nothing reveals so much about God as Jesus; nothing issues from the Bible so clearly as Jesus, who said, "You search the Scriptures, thinking you will find in them eternal life; but they bear witness to me" (John 5:39, AP). No other religion harbors such a crazed, scandalous idea: that God

> apparels himself in common human nature . . . brings good news
> to those who suffer and victory to those who are as nothing; who
> dies like a slave and outcast without resistance; who penetrates the
> very depths of hell in pursuit of those he loves; and who persists

37

even after death not as a hero lifted up to Olympian glories, but in the company of peasants, breaking bread with them and offering them the solace of his wounds. (David Bentley Hart)[1]

Therefore, no other religion is so hopeful, comforting, or challenging, either: for if God has shown himself in this way, in this Jesus, then everything about our lives is forever altered.

The name Jesus was common in first-century Palestine. In Hebrew, *Yeshua* originally was the cry, "Help!" and then, by extension, came to mean "Savior." From the very first generation of Christians, Jesus was called "Christ," which is not Jesus' last name. Christ translates the Hebrew *Messiah*, meaning "anointed one." When a new king assumed his throne in ancient Israel, the climax of the pomp and circumstance came when the priest would pour a flask of precious oil on the head of the new king. This anointing symbolized cleansing for the task ahead, and also that he was empowered by God. But king after king proved to be a disappointment; no one fulfilled Israel's dream for a king wholly devoted to God, zealous for the people of God and their mission. Disappointment transmuted into a future hope: surely someday a great king, a true Messiah will come to lead us, one who will not disappoint.

Several would-be Messiahs appeared during the century when Jesus lived: one named Judas, another also named Jesus, and two named Simon (bar-Giora and bar-Kokhba). All led violent revolts against the Romans; all died ugly deaths. After they died, no one said, "He really was the Messiah." Instead, disappointed followers began to look for another who would prove to be a winner. So you can imagine how Jesus also was a grave disappointment. N. T. Wright wrote that people's expectations for the Messiah

> did not conform to what Jesus did and said, still less to what happened to him. . . . The Messiah was supposed to win the decisive victory over the pagans, to rebuild the temple, and to bring justice and peace to the world. What nobody expected the Messiah to do was to die at the hands of the pagans instead of defeating them, to attack the temple warning of judgment instead of rebuilding it, and to suffer unjust violence at the hands of pagans instead of bringing them justice and peace.[2]

Jesus did not jab his sword at the Romans; he engaged in mortal combat against evil itself, and death was conquered. Jesus built no buildings, but called to himself people, rich and poor, despised and admired, holy and unclean, and declared that the people of God, not any building, would be the embodied presence of God on earth. He called them (and us) to follow him on an adventure we will examine in Lesson 12 when we consider what it means to believe in Jesus Christ as "Lord."

LESSON 11
. . . AND IN JESUS CHRIST (PART 2)

Many have undertaken to set down an orderly account of the events that have been fulfilled among us. (Luke 1:1, AP)

How do we know what we know (or don't know) about Jesus? We have Gospels—something like biographies, although the writers never pretended to be unbiased. They reported events that really took place, drawing out the theological significance of what happened, striving to persuade readers to join the movement set in motion by Jesus. As keenly interested as the early Christians were in what Jesus said and did, he was not (to them) merely the greatest teacher ever, or the most spectacular wonder-worker. Among many great teachers, Jesus alone suffered a horrific death but then did not stay dead. It is Jesus' identity, his horrific suffering but glorious vindication, that define him and our belief in him.

How interesting it is that we have not one, but four Gospels that do not fit snugly together like puzzle pieces should. The four versions are a little jagged-edged, and we might wish we had just one coherent narrative of Jesus' life. But the first Christians preferred the four vivid accounts treasured from the beginning, and so opened themselves to criticism, so obvious were the tensions.[3] But good, deep, meaningful stories are like that. John in particular seems to veer off onto a deeper spiritual plane instead of just sticking with the straight facts; the Fourth Gospel was written "by someone who was a very close friend of Jesus, who spent the rest of his life mulling over, more and more deeply, what Jesus had done, praying it through from every angle, and helping others to understand it. Countless people down the centuries have found that, through reading this Gospel, the figure of Jesus becomes real for them, full of warmth and light and promise" (Tom Wright).[4]

Some popular writers (such as the novelist Dan Brown in *The Da Vinci Code*) have harbored a false picture of how the books of the Bible were chosen, assuming some big meeting was held and a vote taken, and "hidden gospels" were suppressed. Imagine this by analogy: more than one hundred biographies of Thomas Jefferson have been written. We could appoint an "America is good and we must suppress negative thinking about America" committee to decide officially what Jefferson was like. So, biographies that tell of his fathering children by the slave Sally Hemings, or those that show how Jefferson detested the clergy, are to be burned. But this is not how the New Testament came into being. At first, stories of Jesus were passed along word of mouth. Soon, Mark, then Matthew and Luke, and then John were penned, because the first Christians wanted to be certain they had accurate testimony for future generations. They weren't covering anything up; on the contrary, they were doing everything possible to get the word out. But what about the "hidden gospels"? All were written much later (100 to 200 years later) than the four we know. They were not suppressed so much as they simply were not recognized as having even a remote claim to validity.

And it should be said that the "hidden" gospels do not portray a more human Jesus, but a *less* human Jesus. One gospel tells of Jesus in the crib playing with clay, fashioning little birds which he then miraculously causes to fly away. Or his father is in the carpentry shop, and one board is too short, so the toddler Jesus magically lengthens it. One day little Jesus turns his playmates into goats. These stories are clearly legendary, written by people who were not at all comfortable with a human Jesus and wanted him to appear to be as divine as possible. But we will see how mistaken they were about what divinity looks like.

LESSON 12
HIS ONLY SON, OUR LORD

Have this mind among yourselves: Christ Jesus did not count equality with God a thing to be grasped, but emptied himself, taking

> *the form of a servant . . . At the name of Jesus every knee*
> *should bow and every tongue confess that Jesus Christ is Lord.*
> *(Philippians 2:5-11, AP)*

Back in lesson 6, we reflected on Jesus' relationship to God as "Son" of his "Father." But how can we think about Jesus as our Lord? Let us go back to what it means to believe. When people thought the earth was flat, and that the sun, moon, and stars revolved around us, Copernicus stretched his brain outside the presumed paradigm and looked at everything differently: the earth is not the center, we are the ones in motion. Faith involves this same kind of shift. We believe in God, so everything looks different. I am not the center of things; God is. I am the one put in motion, and I see everything from God's viewpoint.

To say "Christ is Lord" is to have the mind of Christ, to think his thoughts, to value his values, to pursue his pursuits. When the first Christians said "Christ is Lord," listeners thought they were crazy, dangerous subversives. For if Christ is Lord, then Caesar isn't! The emperor strutted arrogantly, saying "My will is iron law, nothing else matters, follow my path, buy into my program—or die." And many Christians did; through history, to say "Christ is Lord" has made a dangerous difference.

Do creeds matter? In the 1930s, most German Church leaders were fawning after Hitler and saluting the Nazis as God's instruments. But a handful of defiant believers prayerfully deemed it necessary to unite their voices in a new creed, the Barmen Declaration:

> In view of the errors of the present Reich Administration, we confess these truths: Jesus Christ is the one Word of God whom we have to trust and obey in life and in death. We reject all other powers and historic figures. We reject the false doctrine that there could be areas of our life in which we would not belong to Jesus Christ but to other lords.

One of the creed's signers, Martin Niemöller, then preached a famous sermon—"Christ is my Führer"—and Hitler summarily tossed him in the slammer.

When we say "Christ is Lord," we consciously reject pretenders who claim authority over us, who seduce us away from the way of Jesus. We cannot say "Christ is Lord" without reshuffling our priorities

41

and looking with suspicion at all the world clings to as precious. We discover conflict points; we bump up against the culture; we may suffer for it. Believing and living the truth makes us rather odd, cutting against the grain of a world not committed to Christ.

Jesus came, not so we could feel different, but so we could *be* different. I wonder if this "being different" is where resistance to faith digs in. Søren Kierkegaard put it harshly: "People try to persuade us that objections against Christianity spring from doubt. But the objections against Christianity spring from insubordination, the dislike of obedience, rebellion against authority."[5] He is right, but I like to think of this in more inviting ways: I am moved when I remember the lives of people who have lived as if Christ were in fact Lord. Francis of Assisi's first biographer wrote, "He was always with Jesus: Jesus in his heart, Jesus in his mouth, Jesus in his ears, Jesus in his eyes, Jesus in his hands; he bore Jesus in his whole body."[6] If Jesus is our Lord, we are drawn into a new, exciting, joyful life of service—and we do it together as the Body of Christ, the living presence of Jesus in a world desperately hungry for what only Christ can deliver. Christ is not just my Lord, but *our* Lord, as we are odd together, with Jesus in our hearts, eyes, and hands.

A DEEPER REFLECTION
Are You Down Here?

In *At Home in Mitford*, Father Tim comes to his Episcopal sanctuary one evening just after dark. He doesn't expect to see anyone, but he realizes there's a man sitting in one of the pews. He starts to offer the man some help but notices the man's head is bowed; his prayers gradually become more audible, and finally he lifts his face toward the ceiling, his voice rising to a shrill scream: "If you're up there, prove it!" Father Tim slipped into the pew next to this stranger, and said, "I think the question isn't *Are you up there?* but rather, *Are you down here?*"

I believe in God, the Father Almighty, maker of Heaven and earth, and in Jesus Christ, His only son, our Lord. *Jesus Christ, His only son, our Lord* is the answer, not to the question *Are you up there?* but rather *Are you down here?* As the Nicene Creed phrases it, "We believe in one Lord, God of God, Light of Light, who for us and for our salvation came down from heaven." Jesus came down from heaven. We say he was (and is) God's Son. This belief is neither about his anatomical makeup nor even about the miracles he dazzlingly displayed. Onlookers were awed by his wonder-working, but there were other wonder-workers in those days, many amazements to be soaked in. What was so mesmerizing about Jesus to those who knew him was that he had such an intimate relationship with God. When Jesus prayed, he talked to the powerful God Almighty and called him "Abba," that lovely Aramaic word children spoke intimately while cuddled in their daddy's laps, the name grown men used to express tender affection for their aging fathers. Jesus had that kind of relationship with God his Father. The very name of Jesus (*Yeshua* in Hebrew) means "Lord, help!" Perhaps a woman, after a particularly agonizing labor, would name a son *Yeshua*, echoing her desperate cry just before the child came forth, echoed by the child's first cry as the umbilical cord was about to be cut. "Lord, help!" How perfect that the cry of humanity across the ages is answered by a child whose name is "Lord, help!" Jesus.

He Showed Us His Heart

Are you down here? We believe in one Lord, who for us came down from heaven. How did he come down? In ancient times, believers yearned for a savior who would swoop down, lances blazing, on a chariot of fire. They longed for a savior who would obliterate their enemies, make their gardens grow, and guarantee happiness and prosperity, a savior valiant, mighty, large, muscular, spectacular. But Martin Luther articulated the stunning, humble truth when he said that God became small for us in Christ; he showed us his heart, so our hearts might be won. How odd of God to come as a child—although we may contemplate the personal, humanizing effects a child can have. "A child, more than all other gifts this earth can offer, brings hope, and forward looking thoughts" (William Wordsworth, from the poem "Michael"). When my first daughter was born, I would show her off to the men of my congregation, men who were laborers, with powerful, calloused hands, with gruff, potent voices; and yet the sight of my daughter would soften the hard edges, and they would gently, tenderly scoop her out of my arms into theirs, cooing, making silly sounds in some falsetto. God came down to us, not to outmuscle the world, but to coax us into being tender, loving, soft, even vulnerable. Instead of crushing just one army (even if it had been the legions of Caesar), Jesus battled death itself, and at least seemed to have lost badly. Instead of building a gleaming temple, he called people, rich and poor, respected and despised, pious and unholy, to himself, to be what the temple was supposed to be, the living presence of God on this earth. Instead of turning people's nickels into dimes so they could get rich and prosper, he called that band of people to follow him, to leave everything behind, to risk everything, to be his people, the Body of Christ.

What a disappointment Jesus must have been! And yet, other would-be messiahs had taken their turn at wielding knives and swords, at organizing revolt and seizing power. All wound up dead, and their followers hung their heads and went home. But Jesus, this Messiah, the Christ, suffered the humiliation, the gruesome horror of crucifixion, and yet his followers never returned home, but found themselves catapulted out into the world, energized, zealous. We are here today because something happened to this child who grew up and met an awful end that wasn't really the end at all. Jesus was pronounced "Christ" for the same reason those disciples didn't trudge home in despair: God raised him up from the dead, the Father unable to let his beloved son lie forever in a grave. God came down here for us and our salvation.

To Have Had the Lord on My Mind

So he is our Lord. There is a heavy-handed way to think about Jesus as Lord. We could say Jesus is the boss. He is the autocrat, exercising sweeping control over everything, stepping on any who step out of line. But isn't that how Caesar and his legions were "lord" over the earth? Didn't Jesus say, "You know how those who rule over the Gentiles lord it over them? It shall not be so among you. Whoever would be great must serve. The Son of Man came not to be served but to serve" (Mark 10:42-45, AP). What kind of Lord was Jesus? He was nursed by his mother, Mary; he ate with sinners; he took up a basin instead of a sword and washed the disciples' feet; he opened his arms wide to the world and let them be nailed to a shaft of olive wood. Indeed, as Socrates badgered Callicles into admitting, "If you are serious and what you say is true, then surely the life of us mortals must be turned upside down, and apparently we are everywhere doing the opposite of what we should."[7]

Jesus is not the greatest CEO of all time; if we did a third of what Jesus said we'd run companies into the ground in a week. Jesus is not a cup of coffee to give me a little boost; Jesus is not a fierce manipulator who thrashes bad people and rewards good people. Jesus, this unexpected Christ, is our Lord, working some origami on our minds and the status quo, turning the world upside down.

If God has come down here, if Jesus is Lord, then how do we live? We will always exhibit a kind of disloyalty to the world as it is currently arranged. We will be misfits. We will stubbornly refuse to be normal, to fit in. The form our weirdness will take will be unique to each of us, but at the end of life we will mirror, in faltering ways, the very life of Christ. Near the end of her life, Dorothy Day was interviewed by Robert Coles from Harvard. He thought she was the most remarkable woman of the twentieth century, unsurpassed in serving the poor, speaking prophetically, reminding the Church about courage and compassion. So Coles set up several sessions to capture who she was. In the first he said, "You used to be a writer. Take a notebook, and write some autobiographical reflections about your life; we'll go over them next time when we're together." When they met again, Coles was excited to see what she'd written, but she replied,

> I try to remember this life the Lord gave me; the other day I wrote down the words "a life remembered," and I was going to try to make a summary for myself, write what mattered most—but I couldn't do it. I just sat there and thought of our Lord, and His visit to us all those centuries ago, and I said to myself that my great luck was to have had Him on my mind for so long in my life![8]

Jesus, on my mind for so long: is this how the lordship of Jesus becomes palpable in my life?

We Need Some Help Down Here

Several years ago, one of my associate pastors had a Father Tim moment. A group of homeless people were spending the night in the church. A young woman wandered away from the group and found her way to the sanctuary, where she knelt on one of the altar cushions. My associate happened into the room and, like Father Tim, waited on her to finish praying. Her pleas became more audible, her sobs more pronounced. He headed toward her, thinking to extend a hug or a word, when she screamed toward the ceiling, "God, can't you tell we need some help down here?" Listening to her story, my associate learned that everything in her life seemed to have conspired against her, having suffered abuse, theft, and then the birth of a son she loved but couldn't quite manage. And now they were reduced to sleeping under a bridge. Did she believe in God? She was too desperate not to believe, or even to believe. We need some help down here.

As it turned out, a volunteer spending the night with the homeless people was a lawyer, who realized this young woman had some legal difficulties; she was owed money that would help. So the lawyer went with her to court and helped her develop a budget. Another volunteer, hearing this young mother had no place to live, said "My husband owns a couple of apartment buildings." So she went home and applied proper spousal pressure, informing him he would let this woman and her little boy stay for free for as long as they needed. Others got involved: a dentist fixed a few teeth, a tutor helped the boy get ready for kindergarten, and a businessman gave the mother a job. God came down for us and our salvation. Her prayer was answered, not through a blessing package floated down through the clouds from heaven, but by the joyful action of Jesus, the Body of Christ on earth. Aren't most prayers answerable if we get the divine humor of Jesus coming down like this homeless woman crying out, "Lord, help," and Jesus himself is not just the prayer, but also the answer to the prayer, when we, Christ's Body, cry out. Isn't the way Christ is Lord a beautiful thing?

I keep thinking about beauty—beauty in God's world, beauty in people's lives, beauty in the life of Jesus. His relationship with God his Father was beautiful, as was his affection for Mary his mother, and for the bumbling disciples, not to mention the rich, the poor, prostitutes, and even the smug Pharisees. How mysteriously, ironically beautiful was the cross? And how beautiful is it when the Body of Christ wakes up and sees the answer to prayer? God is not up there. God is down here. Jesus is in our eyes, in our hands, in our hearts. Listen to this lovely reflection from St. Augustine:

Jesus is beautiful in heaven and beautiful on earth. He is beautiful in his mother's womb, beautiful in his parents' arms, beautiful in his miracles, beautiful in inviting people to new life, beautiful in not worrying about death, beautiful in giving his life, beautiful in heaven. Listen to the song with understanding and let not the weakness of the flesh distract your eyes from the splendor of his beauty.[9]

We believe in Jesus Christ, God's son, our Lord, who for us and for our salvation came down from heaven. Thanks be to God.

Notes

1. David Bentley Hart, *The Beauty of the Infinite: The Aesthetics of Christian Truth* (Grand Rapids: Eerdmans, 2003), 126.
2. N. T. Wright, *The Resurrection of the Son of God,* Christian Origins and the Question of God, vol. 3 (Minneapolis: Fortress Press, 2003), 557.
3. William C. Placher, *Narratives of a Vulnerable God: Christ, Theology and Scripture* (Louisville: Westminster John Knox Press, 1994), 87, notes that a bishop in the fifth century discovered people reading Tatian's *Diatessaron,* a harmonization of the four Gospels into a single narrative, and he had the book burned, "striking a blow against repression and in favor of diversity."
4. Tom Wright, *John for Everyone,* part 1 (London: SPCK, 2002), x.
5. Discussed pointedly by Russell Reno, *In the Ruins of the Church: Sustaining Faith in an Age of Diminished Christianity* (Grand Rapids: Brazos, 2002), 53.
6. Thomas of Celano, in *Francis of Assisi: Early Documents,* vol. 1 (New York: New City, 1999), 283.
7. Plato, *Gorgias* 481c. W. D. Woodhead, trans., *The Collected Dialogues of Plato,* ed. Edith Hamilton and Huntington Cairns (Princeton: Princeton University Press, 1961), 265.
8. Robert Coles, *Dorothy Day: A Radical Devotion* (Reading: Addison-Wesley, 1987), 16.
9. Quoted with a lovely discussion in Thomas Dubay, *The Evidential Power of Beauty: Science and Theology Meet* (San Francisco: Ignatius, 1999), 306.

Chapter   Five

CONCEIVED BY THE HOLY SPIRIT, BORN OF THE VIRGIN MARY

LESSON 13
THE VIRGIN MARY (PART 1)

*"You will conceive and bear a son, the Son of the Most High
God." Mary said, "How shall this be, since I have no husband?"
The angel said "The Holy Spirit will come upon you . . .
for with God nothing will be impossible."
(Luke 1:31-32, 34-35, 37, AP)*

I t is hard to visualize Mary apart from the plethora of ways she
has been commemorated in statuary, stained glass, and paintings. Centuries of devotion to her and the dogmas about her
immaculate conception or her assumption into heaven are spiritually zealous attempts to get close to Mary, on the hunch that if we
get close to Mary, we can get close to Jesus.

Think of Mary: not the Mary of later piety, not the Mary hardened
into statue, but the life and blood Jewish girl from Nazareth—
an adolescent, maybe fourteen or fifteen years old, her marriage
(probably arranged by her parents) to Joseph on the horizon, being

interrupted by a mysterious presence. She did not seek what came upon her, but she was open to it. The angel announced the new plan, that her old life was over, that she—really a nobody from no place anybody knew anything about—was to discover in her own body the intersection between God and humanity. Perhaps she could have said no. Instead, she responded, "I am the handmaid of the Lord; let it be to me according to your word" (Luke 1:38). How lovely, how courageous, how single-minded her devotion. As Carlo Carretto put it, "Mary had the courage to trust in the God of the impossible and to leave the solution of her problems to him."[1]

Problems she had: how would Joseph react? what about her parents? neighbors? Would anything ever be the same? or even recognizable? Rowan Williams, the archbishop of Canterbury, wrote these profound words:

> When she first sensed the urgency of God's Word inside her, the longing of God to be here, in this body, her first feeling was a mixture of fear and exhilaration. God had begun to exist in her belly, not through the work of any man, but out of a kind of meeting of her longing and God's. How can anyone carry God? How can you carry the cup without spilling it? But what if the cup is no fragile container but a deep well that can never run dry? Then you know it isn't just your resource, your decision, but God's insistent generosity, carrying you as you carry God.[2]

Then Jesus was born. She heard his first cry, held him gingerly, nursed him, toyed with his fingers, sang to him, and rocked him when he had a fever. She applauded his first steps, swooped him up when he skinned his knee, supervised his household chores, sewed his clothing, laughed and cried with him. She fought back tears when he walked away from home one day. She heard of his exploits, then feared for his life, and finally witnessed a mother's most galling nightmare, weeping at the foot of the cross "while the life's blood she had first given him drained from his wounds and the life's breath he first gasped in Bethlehem escaped in a final cry" (Basil Pennington).[3]

Mary's vocation in life was unique. And yet, like her, we are all asked to offer ourselves to God, to let the very life of God take on flesh right where we are. For the Holy Spirit that came upon her is the same Spirit that brooded over the chaos at creation and brought forth life, caused "dem bones" to rise again (see Ezekiel 37), descended on Jesus at his Baptism (and on us at our Baptism), and rushed on the first disciples (and on the Church in every age), and we are called to respond with nothing less than "I am the handmaid of the Lord; let it be to me according to your word" (Luke 1:38).

LESSON 14
THE VIRGIN MARY (PART 2)

Before Mary and Joseph came together she was found to be with child of the Holy Spirit. (Matthew 1:18, AP)

Among Christians, opinion seems divided on the virgin birth. For many, Mary's virginity is a fundamental belief, without which you are lost; but this cannot be right. We are not saved because we give assent in our brains to the proposition that Mary was a virgin.[4]

For many, the notion of "virgin birth" seems outmoded, unlikely, some hocus-pocus that no longer works for us. If Jesus was miraculously born of a virgin, then Jesus doesn't seem very human, and *The Da Vinci Code*'s raging popularity seems to indicate we rightly crave a connection with a human Jesus. Just as we may not think God created the world in six literal days, some argue that the virgin birth is "merely a metaphor, not even intended to be taken literally," as Joseph Sprague put it.[5] Yet, we may be sure that, whether we accept the virgin birth or not today, Matthew and Luke certainly accepted it as quite literally true.

Interestingly enough, in ancient times, the idea of a virgin birth was relatively familiar and believable to people; Alexander the Great was one of many rumored to have been born beyond mere human copulation. For the earliest Christians, the virgin birth was a way of underlining Jesus' humanity, not his divinity! The shock for ancient people was that anything divine could be born at all; so having a virgin as mother would have been a minimal expectation.

In modern times, science is striving to achieve a kind of "virgin birth" through cloning. But theologically there is a world of difference between a cloned person (should one be born), and Jesus—a difference explained perfectly by Robert Jenson: "A clone would indeed have no father, but not because it was not begotten by human will, but because it was all too much a product of human will."[6] What the Bible is after, even if you have doubts about Mary's virginity, is that Jesus is not merely the product of human action. God is the actor, the protagonist, the initiator in this drama in which we get a direct glimpse into the heart of God through the life, words, actions, death, and resurrection of Mary's son two thousand years ago.

John Shelby Spong is a famous (notorious to many) writer who does not subscribe to Mary's virginity.[7] He believes that medieval notions about women being temptresses and conveyors of evil get layered over belief in Mary's virginity, with disastrous results in society and in the psychological makeup of women, who need to be freed from the fossilized male dominance against which they rightly chafe. I, for one, would say that we have a much more thorny psychological and societal problem, which we will probe in the reflection below.

A DEEPER REFLECTION
Holiness Is Normal

Never have I been asked, "Pastor, do you really believe in Jesus?" or "Do you really believe that he will come to judge?" or "Do you honestly believe in the Communion of saints or the Forgiveness of sins?" Yet frequently I have fielded the question, "Do you really believe in the virgin birth?" A few inquirers just plain wonder, but most fall into two groups, and I wonder if both are missing something crucial. Group One confidently declares, "We believe in the virgin birth. It's one of the pillars of our faith. If people don't believe it, they have no business being in the church." But then Group Two confidently declares, "We don't believe in the virgin birth. We've moved beyond that, it's just a myth—like God creating the world in six days. I can identify with a Jesus born the way I was born, not by magic." In my experience, men weigh in on these questions far more zealously than women, raising a complex issue for another day and another sermon.

When I am pressed, I try to tell the truth that inhabits my particular soul, and with a slight shrug of the shoulders: "I really do believe Mary was a virgin, and that Jesus was conceived by the Holy Spirit. I can't explain the biology of it; I'm not sure I even think of it in a gynecological way, but I do believe it." Reactions to my belief are terribly unsatisfying, at least to me. The adamant defender of the fundamentals of the faith hears this, licks his chops, and pronounces me "fit" to preach, and infers that I must also subscribe to some broad conservative agenda as a result; the modernist debunker of myths grins, a bit paternalistically, perhaps suggesting that "I know you have to say that to keep your job."

Forty or Fifty People

Why do I believe Jesus was conceived by the Holy Spirit, born of the Virgin Mary? And why does it matter? My reasons may seem trivial, oddly oblique, but they are three in number. First (and this is admittedly quirky and not logically persuasive), I thought recently about the forty or fifty people who have lived on this earth that I admire the most: saints, heroes, people whose behavior I wish to mimic, people of whose wisdom, compassion, and prayerfulness I want a small taste. I rambled through their names in my mind, and realized that if someone had asked any one of them, "Do you believe that Mary was a virgin when Jesus was conceived?" every one of them would have said "Absolutely."

This seals nothing, this proves nothing—but I have inherited some kind of community with these saints and heroes. I want a piece of the relationship they enjoyed with God. So if the virginity of Mary mattered to them (to Francis of Assisi, to Mother Teresa, to my grandfather), then believing Mary was a virgin can't be the ruin of me, and perhaps the burden would weigh heavily upon me to dare to venture out in valiant independence from the sacred story that made these people into saints I would emulate. Their thoughts about Mary did not earn them salvation, and not thinking those thoughts can't deprive you or me of salvation; we are saved by the grace of God in this child born to Mary, not by whether we give intellectual assent to his mother's gynecological status. I have no desire to believe on my own. I want to believe in company with those whose lives I would be blessed to mirror in whatever small way. So with them, I believe: Jesus was conceived by the Holy Spirit, born of the Virgin Mary.

Flatlanders

My second reason will appear as ridiculously uncompelling as the first. I asked a friend, who seemed to wave off belief in Mary's virginity as antiquated craziness, "Why don't you believe this?" He said, "There is so much hocus-pocus in the Bible; those miracles worked for prescientific people. But we have science now; we understand how things happen. Humanity has arisen from its prescientific slumbers, and applying our God-given minds to the linkages of cause and effect is our only hope in battling disease and the evils we face. We are responsible for what happens down here." I was tempted to holler "Amen" to that. Carlyle Marney used to say that to be a Christian, you don't have to undergo a lobotomy. God gave us minds, and we barely use a fraction of the cerebral power we have. Or we exercise our brilliance and fritter it away on foolhardy endeavors.

But is everything in our universe simple cause and effect, measurable, manipulatable? Are we entirely responsible for everything that goes on down here? Hearing his words made me shudder, and I stammered after a reply. In college, my dormitory friends and I all read and discussed *One, Two, Three . . . Infinity,* and were intrigued by the notion of "flatlanders."[8] Imagine people who know only two dimensions, left or right, north or south, but were unable to conceive of up and down. If everything is chalked up to human cause and effect, don't we become like flatlanders? And would we not therefore be pitiable creatures? How would we explain the depths, yearnings, resilience, and passion of the people we know and love, much less the complexities of our own souls? Hearing "It's all up to us down here" shoves me into a defensive mode, and I cannot help standing up and declaring that I refuse to live that way.

In hope, I believe there is another dimension, that there is a God, that God loves me and you and the world enough that God gets involved, that God lifts a gentle, powerful finger and dips down into our limited perspective, and does some good. God intervenes. God does things we are not capable of doing. And if God did not do them, we would be lost, we would be lonely, depressive creatures— so I believe in something light years above and around cause and effect, and I pray that somewhere under the encrustations of our modern mind-set every person really does carry around some faint recollection of humanity's pure, original state in the Garden of Eden.[9] I prefer not to be the kind of person who says Mary couldn't have been a virgin because we are so smart and we grasp cause and effect regarding how all babies find their way into the world. Maybe Jesus' birth is the exception that proves the rule. Or perhaps it is the author of this child Jesus' birth that secretly sets in motion the cause and effect that wrought you and me, who are thus not stuck with the fate of the flatlanders.

Does Virginity Matter?

My third reason, I am discovering, is even more important to me at a level I'd have to call "visceral." Someone told me, "The virginity of Mary doesn't matter in modern times," and I found myself responding, "In my opinion, the virginity of Mary matters more in modern times than at any other point in history." I find myself hoping valiantly, pleadingly that Mary was a virgin. Here's why: when Mary bore Jesus, most likely she was fourteen or fifteen years old. And she was not a fourteen or fifteen year old girl in our culture. She was a fourteen- or fifteen-year-old in a culture that attached great shame to having premarital sex. We, however, live in a society that attaches no shame to anything at all. Having sex is mere recreation. Someone spoke of the "normalization" of sex. Someone else spoke of the "McDonaldization of sex": it's like fast food, no big deal. David Brooks trenchantly described life for the young nowadays, who "have no time for serious relationships. They are more likely to go out in groups—and then they hook up for occasional sex." Students he interviewed spoke of having sex "in the tone one might use to describe commuting routes," as the young glibly speak of "buddy sex" among students who distinguish "friendships" from "friendships with privileges."[10] More than half of eleventh graders have had sex with a casual acquaintance. Middle-aged adults seem equally unable to restrain themselves; marriages bust up (or live on) in the face of what we once called "adultery." Turn on the television: people watch as a woman gets sexually involved with ten different guys, and picks the one she likes the most—or a guy does the same with a dozen women. How pathetic. Teenagers and grown-ups who are not sexually active look at themselves and ask, "What is wrong with me? Am I ugly?" We should hang our heads in embarrassment for our species, since our sexual mores basically indicate we are no better than orangutans or rabbits; we simply must satisfy our desires.

Do not think, though, that God is a stiff, anti-pleasure deity. Rather, God the Father Almighty, Maker of heaven and earth, wired us for even higher pleasures, and for deeper joy. God created sex as the most scintillating gift to us, most richly understood when we embrace sex in a lifelong, committed relationship. Regularly, I counsel people whose most gut-wrenching wounds in life have arisen because they frittered away that most precious, intimate part of themselves, squandering their glory with someone who didn't stick around, who didn't love "for better or worse, in sickness and in health." I performed the wedding of a couple last year who had never had sex with anyone; they were virgins. No damage had been done! and they entered their marriage with a profound delight, a sense of pride and integrity, honoring each other (and God!). The Church still has something to say about sexual ethics, not so we might condemn, but because we love people and want only the finest for them. Virginity is not a lack, the missing out on something. Virginity is good.

Sex is not the only holiness issue in our day; we are far more attached to the indulgences of our lifestyle than we are to God. Honesty has slipped under the radar screen in politics, business, and social life. War is an entirely politicized issue, and no one asks much about Jesus or holiness on the international policy stage. But sex may be the vanguard issue with which we must grapple if we would recover a deep relationship with God in the Church; Russ Reno may be right when he says that for modern people who keep their distance from God, "sexual freedom is the crucial line of defense against spiritual demands. . . . It always distracts us from ourselves; modern sexual freedom insists we should do absolutely nothing except to satisfy the immediate demands of our lust."[11]

The Question of Virtue

My hopeful belief that Mary was a virgin is all about my craving for goodness in a sophomoric, hedonistic world. A reporter once pushed his microphone toward Mother Teresa and asked, "Mother, why are you so holy?" She responded, "You talk as if holiness were abnormal. Holiness is normal. To be anything else is to be abnormal. Why aren't you asking unholy people why they are unholy?"[12] Indeed—and can you imagine: "Excuse me, Mr. Celebrity: why are you so unholy?" Good question.

I believe that Mary was a virgin. I hope that that's right. Parenthetically, I suppose some day in God's future we will know for sure. When we talked about God as "maker of heaven and earth," I declared we need not believe God hurled the whole universe and earth into finished form in just six days. Should I die and get to heaven, and God says, "Hey, I really did do it in just six days," I will merely say, "Sorry—but it sure looked like you took longer." If I get to heaven and God says, "Mary really wasn't a virgin," I'll apologize again, but I am going to be very disappointed and, frankly, stunned. For now, down here, we in the Church believe there is still such a thing as goodness, as virginity, as holiness. And to recover the virtues of renunciation, to remember the wonder of the ethical life, to admit like a recovering alcoholic our dependence on a higher power, on a power beyond us, is our last best hope. Everything is not up to us down here. On our own we have that monstrous capacity to be unholy. But we aren't alone down here. God reaches a loving hand down into our lives, into our hearts. God is merciful, and God empowers us to live differently. People say, "Oh, Mary, she's just like everyone else, and Jesus is like everyone else, too." But don't we need a savior who's a little bit different from us? who can show us we don't have to be the way we are, that we can be different? that we can be better?

It helps me in my life to think about Mary. She was a young girl, maturing, full of love and devotion for God. She had plans, a young man, dreams of a home, a family. Then one day in Nazareth, something happened. Did she hear thunder? or was there light? A shadow? or was it the wind? She heard God say, "I have a special task for you. It's going to disrupt your whole life, but you're the one. I need you." And Mary said "Yes." Time passed. Inside herself, she began to feel a stirring, something growing. She didn't understand it, but she knew it was from God. And knowing it was from God enabled her to cope with the rest of her life, for she raised this boy who walked around and spoke of goodness; he was holy. In him, holiness came down here, so we could be holy. People hated him for being holy, and they hurt him—and when they hurt him, his mother's heart was shattered. She watched her holy son's gruesome execution. The only thread you can hang on to in such a moment is to know the child is from God. He was God's Son, he was holy, he was good. When I think about her, and him, they help me to be good. And I need that. We need them. We believe in Jesus Christ, his only Son, our Lord, who was conceived by the Holy Spirit, born of the Virgin Mary.

Notes

1. Carlo Carretto, *Blessed Are You Who Believed,* trans. Barbara Wall (Wellwood: Burns and Oates, 1982), 7.

2. Rowan Williams, *A Ray of Darkness: Sermons and Reflections* (Cambridge: Cowley, 1995), 13.

3. M. Basil Pennington, *Mary Today* (New York: Image, 1987), 14.

4. Even Joseph Ratzinger, before his election as Pope Benedict XVI, wrote, "The doctrine of Jesus' divinity would not be affected if Jesus had been the product of a normal human marriage . . . to confess Jesus as Son of God certainly does not entail denying that he was any other father's son." Joseph Ratzinger, *Introduction to Christianity* (New York: Crossroad, 1969), 208.

5. C. Joseph Sprague, *Affirmations of a Dissenter* (Nashville: Abingdon Press, 2003), 39-40.

6. Robert W. Jenson, *Systematic Theology, Volume II: The Works of God* (New York: Oxford University, 1999), 201 n.79.

7. John Shelby Spong, *Born of a Woman: A Bishop Rethinks the Virgin Birth and the Treatment of Women by a Male-Dominated Church* (San Francisco: HarperSanFrancisco, 1994).

8. George Gamow, *One, Two, Three . . . Infinity* (New York: Viking, 1947), 64-83.

9. Rudolf Bultmann, *The New Testament and Mythology,* ed. Schubert Ogden (Philadelphia: Fortress Press, 1984), 27. This notion of remembrance of a primordial state derives from Plato's *Republic.*

10. David Brooks, *On Paradise Drive: How We Live Now (And Always Have) in the Future Tense* (New York: Simon & Schuster, 2004), 165f.

11. R. R. Reno, *In the Ruins of the Church: Sustaining Faith in an Age of Diminished Christianity* (Grand Rapids: Brazos, 2002), 45-46.

12. *Mother Teresa,* a film by Ann and Jeanette Petrie, Petrie Productions, San Francisco, 1986.

Chapter   Six

SUFFERED UNDER
PONTIUS PILATE

LESSON 15
. . . PONTIUS PILATE

Pilate said to Jesus, "Will you not speak to me? Do you not know I have the power to crucify you?" (John 19:10, AP)

The Apostles' Creed makes a jarring leap straight from Jesus' birth to his death. In *Jesus Christ Superstar,* Judas complains to Jesus: "You've begun to matter more than the things you say." Theologically, he is right: the ultimate significance of Jesus is not his teaching and great deeds. Many teachers have spoken wisely, many women and men have achieved much. For the Creed, the heart of Jesus is unveiled only in his crucifixion. Or we could say that not until Jesus dies and is raised do his words and actions make sense and find their true home.

Jesus was crucified, a horrific form of capital punishment, an excruciating public humiliation designed to intimidate the rabble and keep the peace. The Romans wielded the legal authority to crucify. And they did crucify, and often. The Romans punished the slaves who rebelled under the leadership of Spartacus with mass crucifixions, and many Jews who revolted against Roman authority

THE LIFE WE CLAIM

were crucified, including quite a number under Pontius Pilate. Archaeologists have dug up the remains of a man crucified about the year that Jesus was executed. Interestingly enough, even the Romans regarded Pilate as excessively cruel. With brutal force, Pontius Pilate kept order while he was prefect over Judea for a decade. He offended Jews by siphoning money from the Temple treasury to build an aqueduct, and by marching soldiers into Jerusalem with banners bearing the image of the allegedly divine emperor. Pilate forever reminds us that Jesus was a real person in real history, and that he walked right into the teeth of power and violence.

In Matthew 27 and John 19, we read of the poignant encounter between Jesus and Pilate—a contest between the powerful and the powerless, between steely intimidation and silent humility, between searching questions and silent submission. They converse about truth; it is Jesus, mocked, whipped, a laughingstock, who is the compelling, peaceful servant:

> He was despised and rejected by men; a man of sorrows, and acquainted with grief. . . . Surely he has borne our griefs and carried our sorrows. . . . But he was wounded for our transgressions, he was bruised for our iniquities; . . . and with his stripes we are healed. He was afflicted, yet he opened not his mouth, like a lamb led to the slaughter; they made his grave with the wicked, although he had done no violence. (Isaiah 53:3-5, 7-9)

To the question, "Why did Jesus die?" Christians typically answer, "For our sins." But why did they kill him? Not for their sins! They killed him in the swirl of confusion at Passover, as a million pilgrims flooded the city whose population was usually a mere fifty thousand. Security was an issue, and Jesus had drawn an excitable following, many of whom quite frankly yearned for a militant overthrow of the Romans. And Jesus was the kind of teacher whose pointed words and shocking behavior had a way of making people angry. Jesus—who was a man of peace, innocence, and integrity—was unjustly killed, and Christians have found an immense, profound overflow of meaning in his death. In the next lesson we will weigh the implications of Jesus' suffering under Pilate.

LESSON 16
. . . WAS CRUCIFIED

Jesus said to Pilate, "For this I was born, and have come into the world, to bear witness to the truth." Pilate said to him, "What is truth?" (John 18:37-38, AP)

When Mel Gibson's *The Passion of the Christ* was released, the public focused in an unusual way on the very soul of Christianity: Jesus "suffered under Pontius Pilate." For many of us, the crucifixion is so utterly familiar that we may forget the horror, how brutally gruesome was this execution—and how shocking, offensive, and unexpected the very idea that such a moment could be the wide-open door into the heart of God Almighty.

Rowan Williams compared the story of Jesus' trial to Franz Kafka's *The Trial.*[1] The legal process narrated in the story makes no sense at all. A man named Joseph is arrested without knowing the charge; trying to discover what's up, he violates rules of which he is unaware and finally loses his life in the chaos. No sense can be made of the affair; forces blindly conspire and Joseph is no more. Jesus' trial is akin to this: we cannot discern a logical sequence to the crazed process that begins in arrest and ends in crucifixion, and perhaps we are not meant to discern it. As Albert Schweitzer put it, Jesus flung himself onto the great wheel of history and was crushed by it.[2]

A heated debate resurfaced in the wake of the Gibson movie: who was responsible for Jesus' death? The Jews? The Romans? You and me? The Jews handed him over to the Romans, the Romans handed him back to the Jews, and the disciples handed him over. Hans Urs von Balthasar noticed the truth in this careening handing-over of Jesus: "No one wishes to be responsible. That is why they are all guilty. He rolls like a ball between the competitors, thrown from one to another, held by none, undesired by all."[3] Perhaps, instead of asking "Who was responsible for Jesus' death?" we might ask "Who was forgiven in Jesus' death?"[4]

In the throes of death, Jesus cried out, "My God, why have you forsaken me?" Doesn't this leave us space to cry out in the darkness when we seem forsaken by God? God did not remain safely aloof in heaven, but God entered into human suffering at its darkest. And so in every kind of agony—consider victims of car-bombings, wretched poverty, AIDS across Africa, the numbing agony of marital failure, all kinds of heartbreak, whatever you have faced or will face, and in the hour of your own death—God is there. Just as Jesus stretched out his arms on the cross, so God envelops us in a love that even death could not defeat.

St. Francis prayed before a cross,

> My Lord Jesus Christ, Two graces I ask of you before I die: the first is that in my life I may feel, in my soul and body, as far as possible, that sorrow which you, tender Jesus, underwent in the hour of your most bitter passion; the second is that I may feel in my heart, as far as possible, the abundance of love with which you, son of God, were inflamed, so as willingly to undergo such a great passion for us sinners.[5]

Theologians have debated the inner meaning of the crucifixion, and we may reflect on three ways of understanding its hidden truth. Jesus died as the ultimate sacrifice to bridge the distance between sinners and God: "When we were weak, Christ died for the ungodly" (Romans 5:6, AP). Jesus' death was the climax of God's great grace toward us: "For God so loved the world that he gave his only Son" (John 3:16). And, Jesus was engaged in mortal combat against evil itself: "He has delivered us from the powers of darkness" (Colossians 1:13, AP). God could have achieved all this in countless ways, but how moving, how unique among all the religions of the world, how hopeful that God would do all this for us.

LESSON 17
. . . SUFFERED

We are children of God, fellow heirs with Christ, provided we suffer with him. (Romans 8:16-17, AP)

What else might we discover tucked inside "Suffered Under Pontius Pilate"?

1. For all our modern American talk about the separation of Church and state (or religion and politics), we may reflect on the historical fact that Jesus died at the hands of a politician, and for political reasons. If God is the Maker of heaven and earth, then we cannot erect a fence around some zone of life and tell God, "Hands off!" The prophets of Israel did not shrink before kings, but denounced them when their behaviors or their policies were at odds with God's laws. For two thousand years, Christians have continued this prophetic voice, standing with Jesus instead of endorsing whatever society or the government happens to be doing. The Church refrains from embracing candidates or party affiliations; but we know morality, we know God's vision. We strive to be exemplary citizens; but no government, no politician, not even the best or noblest, can claim our ultimate loyalty.

> The repeated collapse of every earthly imperialism impressively demonstrates that no earthly power can stand forever. . . . God sets up his throne on the wreckage of human earthly thrones, and the history of the world is strewn with the wreckage of demolished imperialisms, whose debris reveals impressively the sole Lordship of God. (Karl Heim)[6]

2. Hidden in "Suffered Under Pontius Pilate" is God's piercing, yet gracious invitation to us to suffer with Christ. Jesus puzzled the disciples when he said, "Take up your cross and follow me." Paul spoke gloriously of Jesus and of our inheritance as God's children, yet added "provided we suffer with him" (Romans 8:17). We may ignore these words, or wish they would go away. We might prefer an intimate, vibrant relationship with God without any sacrifice, without giving up a thing—but it will never happen. If you sense a distance between yourself and God, most likely the problem is that you are hanging on to your stuff, your lifestyle, your arms loaded down with what you prefer to keep for yourself—and you will never get close to God until you learn the beauty of renunciation, until you make genuine sacrifices of your self, your stuff, your time. To get near Jesus, we sacrifice—although when we've done it, we wink, we chuckle, for we notice then that the "cost of discipleship" is nothing compared to the cost of "non-discipleship," that two-bit life that swallows the world's lies that you were made to maximize pleasure and to grab and hang on to all you can get. Jesus suffered so we

might sing, "When I survey the wondrous cross . . . my richest gain I count but loss . . . all the vain things that charm me most, I sacrifice them to his blood. . . . Love so amazing, so divine, demands my soul, my life, my all" (Isaac Watts).

A DEEPER REFLECTION
A Sacrifice That Has Value Before God

Karl Barth rather aptly compared Pontius Pilate's place in the Creed to a mangy dog that wandered unwelcomed into a nice room, smelling up the place.[7] The Creed soars across a vista of grand, glorious, beautiful truths, and then a single mortal man's name interrupts. You would think a stellar disciple or saint would be named. But instead it's Pontius Pilate, a mid-level bureaucrat noted for his cruelty and brutality. He does land in some of the Bible's most dramatic scenes: conversing with Jesus about truth, his wife intervening in the trial to report a haunting dream, theatrically washing his hands.

We may harbor a kind of sympathy for Pontius Pilate. In the movies, from *The Greatest Story Ever Told* to *Jesus Christ Superstar* to Mel Gibson's *Passion of the Christ*, Pilate is torn between duty and a dim discernment of Jesus' innocence. Getting inside Pilate's head seems easy for us, wedged as he is between the proverbial rock and a hard place. How often do we weigh our options, finding ourselves frustratingly shoved into some tough choice, neither option being particularly noble or constructive? But we must choose. Listen to this wise, humbling thought from Richard Holloway:

> The affairs of men rarely allow for a simple choice between good and evil, light and darkness. Whatever you choose to do is wrong, because the whole of our nature is wrong; there is a profound distortion at the root of things which makes all our choices corrupt to some degree. And this was Pilate's dilemma. . . . What is this tragic flaw in humanity that forces us to these decisions? We have turned our backs on the needs of others, because we have other responsibilities. I am Pontius Pilate. Every day I make the unavoidable decision to hand over Christ . . . and he allows himself to suffer at

my hands. These are some of the most momentous words in history. God loves and pities our dilemmas. He has compassion upon our impossible predicaments. He stretches out towards us just as we are: soiled with compromises, heavy with the burden of wrong decisions. He does not hold back till I make the right decisions. He comes to me. He himself becomes the victim of our dilemmas.[8]

Jesus and Politics

Preachers find themselves victims of a complex dilemma. Recently I preached on a huge moral issue, and the congregation's response was resoundingly supportive. Several said, "Oh that was great, we want more of that from the pulpit. We like it when the minister is courageous and takes a stand." I have been preaching long enough, though, to be able to decipher what this kind of praise really means. When the preacher is complimented for her courage, for his stand-taking, the barely hidden subtext is: "I agree with you, and what you said does not affect me personally, does not crowd my lifestyle, does not press me to change." I'm sure you out there listening at this particular service are not this way, but at the other service, and in virtually all the churches, these fair-weather fans will turn on the preacher on the next controversial issue; and instead of saying "Oh that was great, we want more of that," their faces will stiffen. Instead of applauding your courage, they will conclude you are a numbskull; instead of saying you ought to speak out, they say you ought to hush.

Talking about politics in the pulpit draws out a pretty stubborn crowd who think the preacher should hush. "Religion and politics don't mix. Separation of church and state! Can't talk about political things. Miss Manners is wagging her finger at you." But if we can't talk about things political in church, we can't talk about the crucifixion of Jesus, which was all politics. Pilate's job was to keep peace in the Middle East—no easier then than today. Order in the streets called for force, and Pilate never hesitated to deploy force, and we know when force is applied however judiciously, a few innocents are caught in the crossfire. Jesus, indeed, was crushed on the gigantic gears of history, and to this day we utter the name of Pontius Pilate every Sunday—a reminder that Christianity happens in a steely world of politics.

Like the prophets before him, Jesus reveals how God sits in judgment on all things political, that God refuses to be mocked by the powers that be. Pontius Pilate thinks he is judging Jesus. But it is Jesus—isn't it?—who is judging Pilate! Jesus judges every power, every leader, every society, and we who follow Jesus have an absolute obligation to stand with Jesus. Sometimes we may celebrate things that governments and leaders do, but at other times we keep our distance and we offer criticism. A friend, dubious of my patriotic credentials, declared, "Christians are always supposed to support the President." I asked if he supported Clinton during the Monica Lewinsky ugliness. Christians always stand with Jesus, and have no absolute, irrevocable bond to any party, government, or leader—but that's another day and another sermon.

Jesus and Our Suffering

For the Creed only touches on politics. The Creed seems more focused on the far deeper issues of life and death. Jesus suffered under Pontius Pilate, and the Church therefore has forever been the haven where people bear their suffering out loud, where they expect support, where they plead for any hint of hope. We clergy spend time with people who are suffering, who are dying. Sensitive church members will inquire, "How can you do that? That must be so hard. That must wear you out. We worry you will burn out, for you see so much pain and darkness." But sharing in the hour of death, in the darkest hours with another person, is not a burden. It is a privilege. Have you ever held the hand of someone you love when he breathes his last? Have you stuck it out, and her sorrow breaks your heart? You do not regret being present. You see past the horror. You see the tenderness, the nobility of humanity. The dying exhibit a peculiar wisdom, they speak words of profound meaning, they touch with precious affection. Grief itself, which can make your knees buckle, unveils a strange beauty.

When I was eleven, we got a phone call in the wee hours of the morning. The details were cloudy; all we knew was we had to get in the car now, not after sunrise or breakfast, and drive to Oakboro, where my grandparents, to whom I was so intimately attached, lived. Something was wrong with Papa Howell. So my parents piled me and my sister into the car, and we drove through the darkness, into the first light of dawn. We pulled up in front of the house. My father got out and walked up to his brothers standing under the big oak tree. My sister and I, peering through the backseat window of the car, heard no words. Instead these men, who had grown up during the Depression, who worked hard with their hands and served in the armed forces, these powerful men very simply fell on one another's shoulders and cried out loud. My own heart was shattered, but I got a glimpse in their wailing that life is precious, that love is deep, that the worst, most numbing pain is evidence that relationships are profound, everlasting, beautiful.

People often say, "I loved her, and I prayed and I prayed and I prayed for her, but she died. So where is God?" The Creed mercifully reminds us that Jesus suffered under Pontius Pilate. It's not that suffering is over there and God is over here, and we must rush away from suffering to get back to where God is, because where God is there can be no suffering. If you want to find God, look into the face of suffering; visit the place of suffering. Wherever there is human anguish, loss, and pain, God is there. Stand where men fall on one another and cry out loud—and notice the invisible but very strong arms of God surrounding them, holding them up. Jesus suffered under Pontius Pilate. We will never know suffering God has not borne on his own heart: no pain, no tears, no agony God does not know from the inside out, that God has not come into our world to redeem. Jesus suffered under Pontius Pilate.

Provided We Suffer with Him

As a footnote, I might wonder out loud with you if there is not hidden in this truth of the Creed an invitation to us to suffer. We could say, "Christ will bless you, make you feel good, transforming every moment into a party with chocolate cake, your problems all behind you." But this would be a lie, and would rob us of the truest, most penetrating meaning of the Christian life. Jesus did not tell the disciples, "I am going to Jerusalem to suffer, so you run along and have a pleasant life." Instead, Jesus said, "Take up your cross and follow me." In Romans 8, Paul writes so eloquently that we are children of God, heirs of God Almighty; but have we noticed his ominous disclaimer: "provided we suffer with him." We are children of God—provided we suffer with him? Woody Allen said, "I would prefer to achieve immortality without dying." We would prefer to achieve a close relationship with God without suffering for Christ.

A clergy friend of mine reported to me recently that his lay leadership confronted him, chiding him for working too hard. "Go sail a boat, play some golf, relax, take it easy!" was their well-intended counsel. Many of us may well need to learn to relax, but I kept wondering what it might be like if, when we finish this sermon series on the Apostles' Creed, I moved into a new sermon series dubbed, "God wants you to take it easy!" Jesus never said, "Relax, you're striving too hard for the Kingdom of God, you are being too holy, you're too immersed in the Church, you're volunteering too much in service with the poor. Get off your knees. Back off. Take it easy."

Jesus suffered under Pontius Pilate; we are children of God, provided we suffer with him. How little do we comprehend this? A few years ago our church had a food and coat drive. Dashing out the door, I remembered that we'd forgotten to donate anything, so I stuck my head in the pantry and spotted two large cans of sweet potatoes. Perfect! I can't stand sweet potatoes. We'll let some poor person eat them, and we'll feel pretty noble about helping out. Dumping this heartfelt gift in the bin, I noticed a good friend toting an armful of brand new winter coats with the sale tags still attached. "John, what have you got?" John said, "I've been convicted lately by your preaching . . . " and I could see it coming, the humiliating fact that I had not been convicted even by my own preaching. "When I take my children to buy a new winter coat, instead of just giving their old, worn-out, threadbare coats, we buy a new coat for a child. My kids are no better than a poor child, who would really enjoy getting a brand new coat instead of a throw-away." And I hate sweet potatoes?

If you don't feel close to God, maybe you need to hear what Mother Teresa said:

> You must give what will cost you something. This is giving not just what you can live without, but what you can't live without or don't want to live without. Something you really like. Then your gift becomes a sacrifice which will have value before God. This giving until it hurts, this sacrifice is what I call love in action.[9]

Jesus suffered under Pontius Pilate: love in action. We are children of God provided we suffer with him: love in action. Put love into action. Give what costs you something. Do not bring any more sweet potatoes. If you give until it hurts, you will discover the hidden, immense joy of being a child of God. If our church could get serious about giving until it hurts, giving what really costs us something, we could change the world, and people might be lured into believing in Jesus, the one who suffered under Pontius Pilate.

Notes

1. Rowan Williams, *Christ on Trial: How the Gospel Unsettles Our Judgment* (Grand Rapids: Eerdmans, 2000), 3.

2. Albert Schweitzer, *The Quest of the Historical Jesus,* trans. W. Montgomery (New York: Macmillan, 1956), 370f.

3. Hans Urs von Balthasar, *Mysterium Paschale: The Mystery of Easter,* trans. Aidan Nichols (San Francisco: Ignatius, 1990), 115, 118.

4. A wise alternative raised by Dr. Peter Storey.

5. Arnaldo Fortini, *Francis of Assisi,* trans. Helen Moak (New York: Crossroad, 1981), 557.

6. Karl Heim, *The Transformation of the Scientific World View* (New York: Harper & Bros., 1953), 21.

7. Karl Barth, *Dogmatics in Outline*, trans. G. T. Thomson (New York: Harper & Row, 1959), 108.

8. Richard Holloway, *The Killing: Meditations on the Death of Christ* (London: Darton, Longman & Todd, 1984), 26-28.

9. Mother Teresa, *A Simple Path,* comp. Lucinda Vardey (New York: Ballantine, 1995), 99f.

Chapter Seven

HE DESCENDED INTO HELL

LESSON 18
DEAD AND BURIED

Joseph took [Jesus'] body, wrapped it in a clean linen shroud, and laid it in his own new tomb, which he had hewn in the rock. (Matthew 27:59)

We know the crucifixion, Jesus' suffering and dying, and we know Easter, Jesus' resurrection from the dead. But what about the darkest pair of nights and the grief-shrouded day in between, when Jesus was "dead and buried"? While enduring his own bout with cancer (which eventually claimed his life), Alan Lewis wrote a book called *A Theology of Holy Saturday*. Think about it: a 477-page book, all about a day when absolutely nothing happened. The heart of Christianity is focused on a three-day drama, and at the center of the drama is an empty space. Good Friday, the broken heart of God pouring out an immense love on us in the crucifixion of Christ. And then a pause before Easter Sunday, the astonishing news that the tomb was empty, Jesus is risen, life and light unquenchable. In between? Lewis called that Saturday "a significant zero, a pregnant emptiness, a silent nothing which says everything."[1]

We live our lives—don't we?—in-between, like Holy Saturday. Talk to the widow whose husband died of cancer last year. She has seen Good Friday. She may believe the Easter Resurrection is coming—but for now she is in between. Talk to the husband reeling from his wife's exiting their marriage. Talk to anyone trying to cope with living death. We live in between.

Why didn't God just raise Jesus up immediately? The moment they sealed the tomb, God could have crushed the workmen and rolled the stone right back where it came from. But God waited. God did nothing for a time. Perhaps God knew we would experience life and loss and love in just this way. We have hope—but the waiting can be a silent nothing. And we have to wait. We have to hope. We do not get what we long for right now. We live in between.

For the first disciples, Holy Saturday did not feel Holy, any more than Good Friday seemed Good. The day after his death, Jesus was no hero. He was just dead and gone, a tragic failure, and the disciples were crushed by grief. They ambled back into their old existence, unsure what to do next, numb with disappointment. Lewis suggests that God gave us Holy Saturday so we would realize that God is not separate from this kind of unsure, numb, zero emptiness. God knows what it is to weep and linger over a grave. Easter, after all, happened in a cemetery. God was very much present all that Saturday when it seemed nothing happened at all. And God is present on all our Saturdays of sorrow, grief, doubt, devastation. Even that dolorous Saturday really was Holy.

LESSON 19
HE DESCENDED INTO HELL

Christ also died for sins once for all, . . . that he might bring us to God; . . . he went and preached to the spirits in prison, who formerly did not obey. . . . The gospel was preached even to the dead, that . . . they might live in the spirit like God. (1 Peter 3:18-20, 4:6)

The creeds devised by the Church cannot seem to make up their minds: should "He descended into hell" be included or not? The 1 Peter passage seems tantalizingly to suggest that between his burial late in the day on Good Friday and his resurrection on Easter

72

Sunday, Jesus went down into the underworld to save those awaiting judgment. Many New Testament scholars construe the 1 Peter passage differently: if we sort through Genesis 6:1-4, Isaiah 24:21, Jude 6, 2 Peter 2:4, and 1 Peter 3:19-20, we glimpse a belief held by first century Jews, that disobedient angels were thrown into a pit and locked up—and that Jesus' preaching mission was to these evil powers. Still, the Church has historically taught that Jesus "descended into hell"—a doctrine that "need not be explicitly grounded upon specific biblical texts; rather, it must rely upon a reading of Scripture as a whole."[2]

Hell, we know, is not a fiery cavern down in the earth patrolled by red men with pitchforks. Jesus' journey there is symbolic, intimating that all people, in this life and even beyond this life, are offered the love of God. Even the grave does not silence God's call:

> What is to happen to the multitude who lived before Jesus' ministry? And what will become of the many who never came into contact with the Christian message? What is to happen to the people who have certainly heard the message of Christ but who—perhaps through the fault of those very Christians who have been charged with its proclamation—have never come face to face with its truth? Are all these delivered to damnation? Do they remain forever shut out? The Christian faith can say "no" to this urgent question. What took place for mankind in Jesus also applies to the people who either never came into contact with Jesus and his message, or who have never really caught sight of the truth of his person and story. (Wolfhart Pannenberg)[3]

God is relentless, unfazed by time, space, or death itself. Even the pit of hell is owned by the unquenchable love of Christ;[4] the abyss is not bottomless, but has an opening to heaven. Or so many thinkers have argued, unable to make sense of the idea that God could love everyone with infinite power and wind up losing even one. Perhaps Christ's descent into hell opens a window for those who have never heard of Christ, or have heard it from terrible people.

"In view of what Jesus had seen the last few days of his life, maybe the transition to Hell wasn't as hard as you might think" (Buechner).[5] Many theologians have claimed that Christ descended into hell the moment he cried "My God, why have you forsaken me?" on the cross; "No more terrible abyss can be conceived than to feel yourself forsaken and estranged from God, and when you call upon him, not to be heard" (John Calvin).[6] Jürgen Moltmann thought it really began in Gethsemane when Jesus' request that the cup be removed was denied.[7] Whichever side of the grave your hell may be on, "there is no depth, no darkness, no unraveling of reality, which God's Son has not shared" (Nicholas Lash).[8] No matter what hell I go through, God is in the teeth of it with me, descending into whatever abyss I have fallen. And, if Jesus descended into hell, then I as a follower of Christ, and we as the Church of Christ, must follow, and seek out those whose hell is palpable and devastating, and we become the embodied love of Christ for those who think they are totally sealed off from God.

A DEEPER REFLECTION
The Killing Fields

A woman sets the table for two, clinging to her cherished habit despite her husband having died nine months ago. A man lays flowers on a tombstone, conversing at some length with a voice no one else can hear. The wedding ceremony shortsightedly asks for "Till death do us part," as if death were capable of calling a halt to something as fierce as love.

Among mythology's most poignant moments is the heartbreak of Orpheus, who has lost his wife Eurydice. Grief consumes him, as he wanders the earth sobbing and wailing. At length he finds the entrance to the underworld, and manages to get in, descending to the river Styx and the god of death, Pluto, to whom Orpheus pleads: "I have come seeking my wife. Love has led me here. I implore you, I beg you. Unite again the thread of her life. She will eventually be yours, but until then grant her back to me. But even if you deny me this request, know that I will not return without her. You shall have to triumph over us both."[9]

Better Questions

Is this impulse curiously related to all those highly intelligent theological conversations my dorm buddies and I had in the wee hours of the morning, raising what we presumed were titanic questions that were unanswerable, even by God Almighty: What about the people who live in Mongolia (always the country of choice, for reasons that elude me now)? And what about little toddlers who die? Or what about the mentally handicapped? We were so clever, thinking we could stump God—and they are still superb questions that zero in on the very soul of our belief. But we were not quite as clever as we imagined, for we were unaware that God might have anticipated our bafflement. We were unaware that Christian saints and theologians, smarter and wiser than all of us combined, have thought on these matters. We were so very lacking in self-awareness that we did not notice that our very questioning may have been a backhanded stab at keeping God at bay; as long as I keep batting about such tough questions, I can duck God's claim on my life.

Besides, I have better questions now. A few years back, I counseled with a woman who did not believe in Jesus and was a bit hostile to talking about him. When I asked her why, she told her story. Raised in the Church, she went every Sunday and plenty in between. Her father was the prince of Christians, familiar with every nook and cranny of the Bible, a teacher, a deacon, garnering awards for his labors in Christ's vineyard. He was unreserved about his belief in Jesus, his passion for the Kingdom. But those who admired and applauded his piety and humble service were unaware of a private flaw: this very holy man was sexually abusing his daughter through her childhood and teenage years. How unsurprising that as an adult, she wanted nothing to do with her daddy's religion. My question is: who gets saved? The daddy who said, "I believe in Jesus"? Does he get saved? Or does he go to hell? Doesn't the daughter, who says, "I adamantly do not believe in Jesus," get some potent dosage of the mercy of God? Doesn't she get one of the best seats in the Kingdom of God?

What about the people whose only vision of Christianity they have ever heard has been so boringly presented to them? Or what about the people who have heard about Jesus, but from people whose lives are not remotely unique or different from the non-Christian, which leads the listeners to say, "Why bother with a faith so trivial?" What about people who live in countries where Christianity is associated with a foreign country that has bombed the smithereens out of them?

75

So what might we discover at this proposed intersection between love leading husbands and wives to the place where death's door is slammed shut, and the impossible possibility that God has loved but finally lost individuals who had a lousy shot at being found? Like Orpheus, Jesus weeps over the dead. Jesus is heartbroken over a child who is not loved. Jesus yearns for the hearts of those who have never heard of him, who reject him. Jesus' love is so intense, so undeniable, that he not only faced death on the Cross, but invaded the devil's very lair to try to recover those who had died, those he feared were lost.

Disputing Death's Claim

Now, we admit that the geography and geology of this don't cohere for modern people. We know hell is not some cavern so many meters under the earth's surface that spits fire, patrolled by red guys with pitchforks. But the doctrine of Christ's descent into hell isn't a literal travelogue, but a metaphor, a window into the truth of God's heart that transcends up and down, geology and geography, space and time. Like Orpheus, Jesus cannot bear for his beloved Eurydice to be lost; Jesus never promised to love "til death do us part." William Barclay, the great evangelical Bible commentator, said of Christ's descent into hell: "This doctrine means symbolically that either in this life or in life beyond death all are offered the gospel of truth and the love of God. There are no limits in space and time through the grace of God. God has eternity to win us over."[10] What about those in Mongolia? What about the daughter of this very pious daddy? What about those who've been bored to death of what they've heard of Christianity? The answer is, God is not through with them. They're never lost. God continues to pursue them even beyond death itself.

Parenthetically, Americans harbor fascinating thoughts about hell. A Gallup poll indicated that over 80 percent of Americans believe there is a hell—more than two times the number who attend church! When I was in college, I was familiar with the usual view of hell, the fiery pit and Satan's red henchmen with pitchforks, which I recognized as crass silliness; but then someone handed me C. S. Lewis's *The Great Divorce*. Lewis, I was to find out later, was clever on the subject of hell: when asked, "Do mosquitoes go to heaven or hell?"

he wryly answered, "Well, there is a heaven for mosquitoes, but it's the same place as hell for people." In *The Great Divorce*, Lewis imagines hell as a dingy, dark place, the weather always overcast. People mull about, hanging their heads, depressed in this bureaucratic nightmare of a place. Curiously, they can leave at any time, but they prefer to stay in hell. Accustomed to the place, they stay, relishing hell's activities calendar, including theological discussion groups where they talk about questions like what happens to people in Mongolia. Lewis provides us with some short quotations from hell's residents: "I don't want any help. I want to be left alone. I'm in charge of my own life"—common sentiments in hell. As Lewis surmises, "There is always something they insist on keeping, even at the price of misery. There's always something they prefer to joy. There are only two kinds of people in the end. Those who say to God, 'Thy will be done.' And those to whom God says, 'Thy will be done.' And all that are in hell chose it."[11]

Whether Lewis's image of a hell you can leave at any time suits your sense of theological truth or not, you must decide over lunch. We may contemplate James Kay's wise words: "If death were an impenetrable barrier for God's redeeming grace, then death would be God. Death would have the final word. Christ's descent into hell disputes this claim of death to absolute lordship."[12] As Christians, whatever we may believe about hell and its future citizenship, we have absolutely no option but to hope passionately for, to pray zealously for the salvation of every person, and to grieve over the very idea that even one might perish.

Visible Branch Establishments

Here is something that seems undebatable: If Jesus descended to hell, we are called to follow him there. I heard an angry man say, "The Church can go to hell!" *Can?* We *should*, we must. Hell is not merely on the far side of the grave. Robertson Davies wryly said, "There's no reason why hell should not have, so to speak, visible branch establishments throughout the earth, and I have visited quite a few of them."[13] I have, too, as have you, and maybe we will never get very close to Christ until we launch out on a major itinerary to visit a few more. Go to the ancient city of Bam, where 50,000 Iranians were killed in the earthquake. Go to the West Bank, where children dare not go out of the house, except it's not safe in the house either, as they grow up in apartment buildings that have been shelled repeatedly. Go to Kenya where AIDS ravages the population. Go to Manhattan or Connecticut, to a condominium where children do not have a mom any longer, not since September 11, 2001, the day mom never came home from work. Go just two and a half miles from this lovely neo-Gothic sanctuary and see what life is like across the tracks in our major league city of Charlotte. Look around at our culture, polluted by decadence and shamefulness, sexuality run amok. Sit in the waiting room with the parents whose pediatrician has just announced their daughter has a brain tumor. Visit your neighbor whose "darkness visible," depression, shackles him to a chair; or look across the dining room table at the one you love but cannot quite understand. Visible branch establishments of hell.

Christ descended into hell. Thank God. "If the Lord had not been on our side, we would have been swallowed whole" (Psalm 124:2-3, AP). And the same Jesus who descends to every branch establishment of hell asks us to follow him, not at a safe distance, but up close. The Christian's "place" is not in the lovely, safe confines of the church building, but out in those visible branch establishments. Just as Jesus invaded the devil's lair, so we dare to insert ourselves into places and situations that seem godless. But because Jesus descended into hell, we know there is no such thing as a godless place. Whenever we as the Church go to hell, we find that Jesus is there ahead of us, and we discover that we at long last are actually close to the Jesus for whom we long.

We never underestimate the power of Jesus in those visible branch establishments of hell. I have a friend, my shortest clergy colleague, just a small man, but only in physical stature. Sam grew up in Cambodia, in the "killing fields," where bombers, napalm, and guerrilla warriors conspired to pillage his beautiful country, reducing it to ashes. Sam was cynical, his hope burned beyond recognition. Somebody gave him a Bible. As a Buddhist who was reared an atheist, he was trying to survive, and this Bible came in handy, as he needed papers to roll his cigarettes. Tearing out page after page, smoking his only indulgence, Sam became very attached to his Holy Bible. He rolled through Genesis, Exodus, the stories of Samuel, Saul and David, Ruth and Naomi, the Psalms, the prophets, into the New Testament. Bored, he tore out the first page of the Gospel of John, read it, rolled up the cigarette, and smoked it: "The Word became flesh, full of grace and truth," up in curling smoke. Second chapter, he read, rolled, and smoked: water into wine at Cana, Jesus hurling the moneychangers out of the temple, smoke rising. He came to the third chapter, tore the page out, read, started rolling, but then he unrolled the page, read it again. "For God so loved the world, that he gave his only begotten Son, that whoever believes in him should not perish, but have everlasting life." He stuck the page in his pocket, found a chaplain and asked, "What is this? Tell me more." The rest is history—Sam's story of becoming a Christian and then a minister; God's story of descending into the hell of Cambodia's killing fields to rescue the lost; the story of the Church going to hell to save one very short, lightweight man, who has had significant ministry in the country that used to send bombers over his head, and now is going back to those killed fields to share the Gospel with his native countrymen.

We do not follow Christ safely behind these stone walls. God calls us to follow Jesus into the teeth of evil itself, to find the lost, those who do not believe. And we dare not bore them, or live lives where our faith is only pasted superficially on the outside. Jesus goes to hell, and if we love him and want to be near him, we, too, go to hell, trusting that hell itself now belongs to Jesus, the abyss miraculously transformed into a road (Gregory the Great's image), Dante's "Abandon hope, all who enter" sign torn down. You may not get credit; no one may be watching, but then no one could see Jesus on that Friday night and long dismal Saturday.[14] The closer we stay to Jesus, the more we notice his invisible work, the more we love those he loved, the more we find ourselves in ugly places—which are no longer ugly, for Christ is there. We the Body of Christ are there, and the imprisoned souls are set free.

Notes

1. Alan E. Lewis, *Between Cross and Resurrection: A Theology of Holy Saturday* (Grand Rapids: Eerdmans, 2001), 3.

2. David Lauber, *Barth on the Descent into Hell: God, Atonement and the Christian Life* (Burlington: Ashgate, 2004), 112.

3. Wolfhart Pannenberg, *The Apostles' Creed in the Light of Today's Questions*, trans. Margaret Kohl (Eugene: Wipf and Stock, 1972), 94-95.

4. James F. Kay, *Exploring and Proclaiming the Apostles' Creed*, ed. Roger E. Van Harn (Grand Rapids: Eerdmans, 2004), 118, observes that "the Creed speaks of hell with reference to Jesus Christ. Hell only appears in relation to him. Whatever hell may turn out to be . . . it cannot be confessed independently of Jesus Christ. He did not evade hell. He entered into it."

5. Frederick Buechner, *Whistling in the Dark: an ABC Theologized* (New York: Harper Collins, 1988), 37.

6. John Calvin, *Institutes* II.xvi.10.

7. Jürgen Moltmann, *The Trinity and the Kingdom: The Doctrine of God*, trans. Margaret Kohl (Minneapolis: Fortress, 1993), 77.

8. Nicholas Lash, *Believing Three Ways in One God: A Reading of the Apostles' Creed* (Notre Dame: University of Notre Dame Press, 1992), 60.

9. Edmund Fuller, ed., *Bulfinch's Mythology* (New York: Dell, 1959), 151.

10. William Barclay, *The Apostles' Creed for Everyman* (New York: Harper & Row, 1967), 127.

11. C. S. Lewis, *The Great Divorce* (New York: Macmillan, 1946), 60, 69, 72.

12. Kay, *Exploring and Proclaiming the Apostles' Creed*, 127.

13. Robertson Davies, *Fifth Business* (New York: Penguin, 1970), 46.

14. Lauber, *Barth on the Descent into Hell*, 168; though of "the unseen form of Jesus Christ's non-violent love in his burial and descent into hell. Effective suffering and non-violent enemy-love is not restricted to those cases that are well-publicized and honoured for dramatic heroism. Even those instances of overlooked or unknown suffering significantly participate in and bear witness to God's transforming love for the world."

Chapter Eight

THE THIRD DAY HE ROSE FROM THE DEAD

LESSON 20
THE THIRD DAY . . .

He has risen, he is not here. (Mark 16:6)

M any philosophically minded people have suggested that the resurrection of Jesus cannot be historical, if by "historical" we mean events we can comprehend within the normal course of cause and effect, events that are measurable, understandable, explainable. The much-publicized Jesus Seminar even held a press conference with a mortician to prove dead people don't rise. The first Christians would agree: the immeasurable, the inexplicable, the impossible happened. Jesus was dead and buried by sundown Friday—but on the third day (Sunday morning) his tomb was empty, and not by theft or deception, for Jesus himself appeared to some women, and then to his disciples, who were so transformed by meeting him that these unlettered fishermen were catapulted onto the world stage where they quite literally changed the world.

Charles Colson once argued that the story of the resurrection must be true, since even a smaller number of Watergate crooks couldn't keep their stories straight and wound up exposing Nixon as a liar.

Therefore, to Colson, had the resurrection been fabricated, some bumbling disciple would have leaked the information. Jürgen Moltmann has a point: "The message of the resurrection brought by the disciples on their return to Jerusalem could hardly have lasted a single hour in the city if it had been possible to show that Jesus' body was lying in the grave."[1]

Surprisingly, almost embarrassingly, several stories—seemingly self-contradictory, and not at all "kept straight"—were allowed into the Gospels. Who really got to the tomb first? and to whom did Jesus appear? Did he appear just outside the tomb? or was it up in Galilee? The four narratives of the resurrection do not fit together very easily. These variant stories virtually beg critics to scoff. We almost wonder if the resurrection were so contradictory to life as we know it that the feeble efforts to put it into words inevitably seemed crazed, just as Luke characterizes the reaction to the women's breathless report of the empty tomb: "These words seemed to them an idle tale, and they did not believe them" (Luke 24:12).

The philosopher Ludwig Wittgenstein once asked why these texts were so unclear. He compared the situation to someone wanting to warn people of a terrible danger, but telling them a riddle. "Isn't it possible that it was essential in this case to tell a riddle?" Wittgenstein wisely asked, as if a riddle were the clearest way to convey this particular kind of truth.[2] An empty tomb. Conflicting accounts. Rumors of meetings. Doubts, surprises, but a powerful message. This Jesus—itinerant preacher, quiet healer, offense to the pious, scandalously executed—could not be contained by the grave, and this wonder was so fantastic that it could not be corralled into straight, manageable, logical accounts. Certainly if the early Church made this up, they would have guaranteed that the four Gospels were in airtight agreement.

LESSON 21
. . . HE ROSE FROM THE DEAD

If Christ is not risen, our faith is in vain. (1 Corinthians 15:14, AP)

When we speak of the resurrection, we do not mean that Jesus' soul survived the death of his body, and yet we do not mean the mere resuscitation of a corpse. The risen Jesus is not recognized, but then is recognizable. He can be touched, but then he pulls back. He materializes, and then he vanishes. Paul spoke of the resurrection as involving a "spiritual body" (1 Corinthians 15). A body, yes, but spiritual, not merely a spirit, but a body, totally transformed, animated entirely by the Spirit, not liable to disease or death. So for those whose understanding of anatomy makes a resuscitation seem ridiculous, the Bible narrates something different, and far better—better even than the immortality of the soul. The Bible promises the resurrection of spiritual bodies. We can rejoice, even if we lack clarity on this matter: "The Church binds us to no theory about the exact composition of Christ's Resurrection Body" (Dorothy Sayers).[3]

Perhaps for those who read the Bible's stories of Jesus' resurrection, the most surprising discovery:

> It is extremely strange, and extremely interesting, that the stories of Jesus' resurrection never mention the future hope of the Christian. . . . Instead, we find a commission *within* the present world: "Jesus is risen, therefore you have work ahead of you." The stories are about the vindication of Jesus, the validation of his claims, and the commissioning of his followers to act as his heralds, announcing to the world its rightful lord. (N. T. Wright)[4]

A reporter asked me, "Do you believe the resurrection really happened?" I do not believe a corpse was resuscitated, but I most certainly believe Jesus was resurrected by God, that he was transformed into a spiritual-bodily existence and appeared to the disciples, and lives today. Frederick Buechner said it beautifully:

> We may try to say that the story of the Resurrection means the teachings of Jesus are immortal like the plays of Shakespeare or the music of Beethoven. Or we can say that the Resurrection means the spirit of Jesus is undying, that he lives the way Socrates does in the good he left behind. Or we can say the language of the Gospels is the language of poetry and that it is not to be taken literally but as pointing to a truth more profound than the literal. We try to reduce it to the coming of spring, or the rebirth of hope in the despairing soul. We try to suggest that these are the miracles the Resurrection is all about, but they are not. They are all miracles, but they are not this miracle. If I believed this was all the Resurrection meant, then I would turn in my certificate of ordination and take

up some other profession. Or at least I hope I would have the courage to. The Resurrection is proclaimed as a fact: Christ is risen! Unless something very real took place, there would be no Church, no Christianity.[5]

Or as John Updike, of all people, put it nearly fifty years ago:

Make no mistake. If Jesus rose at all, it was as his body. It was not as the flowers. It was not as his spirit. It was as his flesh, as our flesh. The same hinged thumbs and toes. The same valved heart that pierced, died, withered, paused and then regathered out of enduring might new strength to enclose. Let us not mock God with metaphor, analogy, side-stepping transcendence, making of the event a parable, a sign painted in the faded credulity of earlier ages. Instead let us walk through the door. The stone is rolled back. Not a paper maché stone, but the vast rock of materiality that in the slow grinding of time will eclipse for each of us the wide white of day. Let us not seek to make it less for our own convenience, our own sense of beauty, lest awakened in one unthinkable hour we are embarrassed by the miracle.[6]

A DEEPER REFLECTION
An Empty Place

Matthew Arnold, in "Dover Beach," wrote that the sea of faith

Was once too, at the full, and round earth's shore
Lay like the folds of a bright girdle furl'd.
But now I only hear
Its melancholy, long, withdrawing roar,
Retreating, to the breath
Of the night-wind, down the vast edges drear.

Turn to most any other writer worth reading, and you overhear echoes of that same withdrawing roar, the same empty place where faith is supposed to be, where faith perhaps once was, but is no more. Paul wrote that "if Christ is not raised, we are to be pitied," but even pity is pointless. The preacher wishes she could fill up that vacuum; he fantasizes that one day the sermon will kick into over-drive and even the grittiest skeptic would rush to the altar professing belief.

Personally, in my own life of faith, I find it richly appealing to stake everything on the reckless absurdity that my life is not just this lone entity with some invisible due date stamped on it, for I believe that history pivoted when a tomb outside Jerusalem turned up empty, and Jesus turned up in his fullness. I find it compelling to consider that the disciples, not an imaginative, creative bunch, with everything to lose, did what no other people who had been swayed into following a would-be Messiah (and there were plenty of them) around the countryside had done: instead of hanging their heads and trudging home, or looking behind the next rock for a better messiah, they plunged headlong out of the city, away from family and home, breathlessly, giddily telling the preposterous story that Jesus was indeed alive and glorified, risking (and losing) life and limb, intrepid voyagers traveling where they were incapable of going, but getting there, getting to us.

It's Not About Me

The sea's withdrawing roar. An empty place where faith used to be. We brilliant, clever modern people: are we the culprits who hollowed out the empty place by deciding that "I am the arbiter of truth; I can trust only myself, I decide what is true and what is not true, and if it doesn't suit me then it's not true"? When Mel Gibson's movie *The Passion of the Christ* came out, I was peppered with the question: Is it factual? That's so American, isn't it (and a bit much to expect from Hollywood)? We want the facts. Isn't it all about control, being in charge? I do not blame you if you feel this way, for you and I grew up in a culture that has tutored us to take charge. It's all up to you. Mess up, it's your fault. Succeed, pat yourself on the back. But isn't this a lonely, harsh existence? When the Creed declares, "On the third day, he rose from the dead," the message is: it's not all up to you. It's not all about you. There is a power beyond what we can control, beyond what we can imagine, beyond my small-minded proof or suitability.

How fascinating that the Gospel stories of Jesus' resurrection say nothing at all about me, my death, or life beyond death. When this was first pointed out to me, I actually had to rummage back through the Bible's pages to check. Surely there is something in this for me; surely the angels at the tomb said, "He is not here, so do not be anxious when you die, you will not be stuck in the grave either; you'll enter the pearly gates and be with Jesus and those you love." For Matthew, Mark, Luke, and John, the "point" of the story seems to be not that you, too, can be raised from the dead—or if this is their intent, they do a lousy job of explaining things! Again: how typically American of us, to turn the story of God raising Jesus into something for me, something I can consume, something I can get in on.

The third day he rose from the dead: this tells me nothing about me, but everything about God. The resurrection of Jesus is a mass of trumpets announcing that God is God, that Jesus really was the Messiah, that the Lord of the universe has just left a large signature on this planet, that inexplicable power resides in God's arm, that God's love triumphs over every dark foe, even death itself. God is glorified. God be praised. Dietrich Bonhoeffer understood this, and his belief in this powerful, loving, unvanquished God won him a stiff concentration camp sentence and execution by the SS. While imprisoned at Tegel, he wrote that our life with God is "not in the first place thinking about one's own needs, problems, sins, and fears, but allowing oneself to be caught up into the way of Jesus Christ."[7] Getting swept up in something greater than myself: this is what you and I are hungry for, and yet isn't identical with my hunger. It's happening, even if I refuse to join the party.

The Empty Space

A friend visited Neils Bohr in his office one day and noticed a horseshoe affixed above the door. "What's this?" Bohr replied, "A lucky horseshoe." The friend said, "You are a physicist; surely you're not a superstitious person." Bohr said, "I'm not superstitious. However, I am led to believe that this horseshoe works whether you believe in it or not." I have tried lately to think about things that work whether you believe in them or not—and there are many. Isn't "on the third day, Jesus rose from the dead" one of them, the most important of all, the only one that finally matters? The curious unfolding of the resurrection story begins with an empty tomb. No one saw any pyrotechnics; no one witnessed Jesus emerging from the grave. The tomb was empty. The place where God acted left no telltale signs, no traces of atomic waste left behind. Just an empty space. We might prefer to think that where God acts, there is plenty to see, containers are filled, cups overflow. But the first evidence, the first location of God's greatest act is an empty place.

Perhaps this is where we can climb on board this adventure. Without psychologizing the resurrection too much, we can all admit that we have a hollow place inside. Even if I have faith, a gnawing emptiness dogs my happiest moments. Typically we sense this hollowness as an evil to be fled. We feel empty, and we rush out to fill the space with something, anything: busyness, booze, diversions, stuff. For years I have said we can fill that space with God and not feel empty any more. But those were superficial sermons I delivered, short-circuiting God's intended, deeper process for me and you. That cavernous space where the cold wind seems to blow through my soul need not be viewed as an evil to be avoided, something lacking, a problem to be solved quickly. Perhaps that space was put there by God. When I feel the hollowness, when I sense something big is missing at the heart of my life, I do not flee, but I stay, I listen, and I recognize in that hollowness the very voice of God calling to me, reminding me that I belong to the God whose first and finest achievement was an empty place.

If "on the third day, Jesus rose from the dead" is in some way about my death and the loss of those I love, then maybe we stick with the hollowness here too. I have a friend whose daughter died in a terrible car accident, an aunt whose son died from a freak infection, a friend whose husband succumbed to colon cancer, a neighbor whose mother suffered from Alzheimer's and then just faded into the darkness. They are like you and me: we have all loved, and lost, and there is a painful gap where that person used to be, a haunting empty chair when family photos are taken nowadays, a dark glimmer in the soul. Pious people, so eager to help, lean in to say, "God can fix how you feel; God can cure your hurt; God can fill the gaping wound."

But I shall never forget the first time (and luckily, the last time) I tried such an ineffective balm on a father whose daughter had died suddenly. Pitifully I tried to say, "God can help you feel better," but he firmly but calmly told me, "I don't want to feel better." I dimly understood that the pain is an index into the depth of the love, and so to ameliorate the pain might risk a diminishing of the love, or to move on and feel better might cloud the memory.

Bonhoeffer again, who understood sitting alone in an empty stone place, thinking on Christmas Eve 1943 of family he had loved and lost, and no doubt of his own fate and awful separation from his beloved family, wrote these jarring, eloquent words from his prison cell:

> Nothing can make up for the absence of someone whom we love, and it would be wrong to try to find a substitute; we must simply hold out and see it through. That sounds very hard at first, but at the same time it is a great consolation, for the gap, as long as it remains unfilled, preserves the bonds between us. It is nonsense to say God fills the gap; he doesn't fill it, but on the contrary, he keeps it empty and so helps us to keep alive our former communion with each other, even at the cost of pain. . . . The dearer and richer our memories, the more difficult the separation. But gratitude changes the pangs of memory into tranquil joy. The beauties of the past are borne, not as a thorn in the flesh, but as a precious gift in themselves.[8]

He Is Not Here

An unfilled gap. A space for memory. Come to think of it, isn't the Church just such a space held open so we might remember? We want the Church to be something solid, substantive, full of activity, bustling with Sacraments and teaching and noble do-gooding. But anyone who has been in the thick of Church life knows how bumbling, fumbling, and teetering on the edge of silliness we are at every moment. The Church fails in its mission, and miserably. But the very failure can open up some kind of space for bumbling, fumbling, silly people to back into their place with God. Karl Barth understood the Church as an empty, hollow space,

> a canal through which flows living water. Wherever graves are, there is resurrection. Where the church ends, there is its beginning. Where its unrighteousness is exposed, there its righteousness dawns. The divine demolition of any Church means that every Church arises as a signpost, threshold, and door of hope. . . .

Broken, the Church can bear its message with its head erect, for the Gospel belongs to the Church that is lost.[9]

Our life is not lived in the immediate, direct, palpable, tangible presence of God. "He is not here; he is risen." We love the "risen," and forget that "he is not here." Imagine how devastated, how emotionally jolted the disciples must have been, giggling with glee that Jesus was back, that he was alive once more, when he informed them that it was only for a very brief time and that he would be going soon, returning to his Father in heaven, leaving them here, alone again. Like parents who dote on their children, but love them too much to cling to them forever, Jesus walked away, and the strangest of all God's acts was precisely that departure, trusting the not so very trustworthy disciples to stand on their own two feet, to carry out a commission to transform the world. On the third day he rose again, ascended into heaven. We might prefer he had stayed, so we could hold hands, so he could keep his arms around me every moment, so he could dash off a miracle or two when required. But how like God the Father is this Jesus: just as he left the tomb empty, he leaves this earth and our lives empty, not full, with a space that lingers, a space that can hurt, a space that can remember, a space in which we can get to work. For our life is forever defined by an empty place, an open space, and is lived best when we keep it empty and open—which is the impossible possibility. It works whether you believe in it or not.

Notes

1. Jürgen Moltmann, *The Way of Jesus Christ: Christology in Messianic Dimensions*, trans. Margaret Kohl (Minneapolis: Fortress Press, 1993), 222.

2. As discussed by William C. Placher, *Narratives of a Vulnerable God: Christ, Theology, and Scripture* (Louisville: Westminster John Knox Press, 1994), 91.

3. Dorothy L. Sayers, *Creed or Chaos? Why Christians Must Choose Either Dogma or Disaster* (Manchester, N.H.: Sophia Institute Press, 1995), 11.

4. N. T. Wright, *The Resurrection of the Son of God* (Minneapolis: Fortress Press, 2003), 602.

5. Frederick Buechner, *The Magnificent Defeat* (San Francisco: Harper & Row, 1966), 77f.

6. John Updike, "Seven Stanzas at Easter," in *Telephone Poles and Other Poems* (New York: Random House, 1963), 72-73.

7. Dietrich Bonhoeffer, *Letters and Papers from Prison*, ed. Eberhard Bethge (New York: Macmillan, 1972), 361.

8. Ibid., 176.

9. Karl Barth, *The Epistle to the Romans*, trans. Edwyn C. Hoskyns (London: Oxford University Press, 1968), 375, 416.

Chapter Nine

FROM THENCE HE SHALL COME TO JUDGE THE QUICK AND THE DEAD

LESSON 22
HE ASCENDED INTO HEAVEN

"You shall receive power when the Holy Spirit comes, and you shall be my witnesses in all the earth." When Jesus said this, he was lifted up, and a cloud took him out of their sight.
(Acts 1:8, AP)

For people in Bible times who thought of the world as a flat surface, with heaven as a chamber up above the clouds, the story of Jesus ascending seemed entirely natural. For modern people, "up" loses its meaning after so many miles, and telescopes peer far beyond what biblical people imagined as the "top" of heaven.

So how do we make any sense of "He ascended into heaven"? If we were correct in lesson 21 when we said the resurrection was not the resuscitation of a corpse, but that Jesus was raised with a "spiritual body," then we don't have an insurmountable intellectual problem. Jesus "appeared" and then was gone; his appearances lasted for forty days (a point on which all the first Christians were in agreement), and then they stopped. Jesus was gone; yet he was exactly where we would expect him to be: at the side of the God with whom he had spoken so intimately on earth. Jesus could be nowhere else but in heaven, which for us need not be a place an astronomer could pinpoint—and perhaps for that very reason is the fullness of togetherness with God.

In *The Lord of the Rings,* the wise, old Christlike wizard Gandalf is with the hobbits for a while on their adventure, but then he leaves them on their own for some time. They face horrific difficulties, requiring ferocious courage and intense hope; they need one another and stick together in a fellowship that would rather suffer than falter. Gandalf shows up again at the climax, but then bids them farewell once more. The Bible narrates a story with a kindred plot line. Jesus heals, teaches, dazzles, confuses, suffers, and then is raised—and then he leaves. What a demonstration of trust! And what a challenge for us! Instead of dominating his people, instead of insisting that they never get out from under his heels, he leaves them on their own. But they are not alone. As Jesus ascended, he said "Lo, I am with you always!" (Matthew 28:20). He had promised: "I will send the Spirit, the Comforter, who will guide you into all truth" (John 14). The Christian life leaves considerable room for us to make our own way. Courage, hope, and fellowship are essential. We remember Jesus, we embody what he was about, and even though he isn't tangibly in front of us, his Spirit moves us, motivates us, encourages us in his absence.

For we have work to do. When Jesus "leaves," the book of Acts tells us what the Christians did next: they continued "what Jesus began doing" (Acts 1:1-9, AP). This is the Christian life and the life of the Church! We are the continuation of what Jesus began doing. We are the Body of Christ. "Christ has no body now on earth but yours. . . . Yours are the eyes through which the compassion of Christ looks out on a hurting world; yours are the feet with which he goes about doing good; yours are the hands with which he is to bless now" (Teresa of Avila).[1]

Theologically, the ascension of Jesus to God the Father blazes the trail on which we are blessed to follow. "Let us run with perseverance the race that is set before us, looking to Jesus the pioneer and perfection of our faith, who . . . endured the cross, . . . and is seated at the right hand of God" (Hebrews 12:1); "God, rich in mercy, even when we were dead through our trespasses, made us alive together with Christ and raised us up, and made us sit with him in the heavenly places" (Ephesians 2:4-6, AP). Indeed, Christ came, not so he could be like us, but so we could become like him, and enjoy the beauty of togetherness with God forever.

LESSON 23
HE SHALL COME TO JUDGE . . .

Repent! for God has fixed a day when Jesus, whom he has appointed, will judge the world, and of this he has given assurance to us by raising him from the dead. (Acts 17:30, AP)

"Judge not," as Jesus told his disciples—and we may imagine him adding, "because you don't have to." What a relief! However much we may savor a critical thought, pronouncing our small-minded sentence of judgment on someone who either is different from us, or curiously enough embodies our own foibles. Judgment belongs to God, not to us. Yes, we must make judgments, we must reflect wisely on right and wrong, and decide as individuals, and together as people, where lines are to be drawn. But we need not, for we cannot, sit in judgment on any other person.

But this does not mean there is no judgment. Jesus will come to judge the quick and the dead. Without judgment, life is emptied of all meaning; without judgment, morality is a sham. We had best hope there will be a reckoning for evildoers. And we had best hope there will be a reckoning for us, too. For all are judged—not just the obviously wicked. God is not like Santa Claus, jotting down the names of who's naughty and who's nice. Saint Francis of Assisi and Mother Teresa lived in recognition that at the end of their lives they would be assessed, measured for all they had done and thought. Judgment is not just at the end of time, though. There is a judgment happening every day, in fact at this very moment as you read—as well as last night, this evening after dinner, tomorrow morning.

God is nosy, getting inside your head, peeking behind doors and under rugs, weighing thoughts, motivations, little dark urges we would prefer not to notice. God rattles around inside your body, knowing what you put in it, where you take it, what you do with it. Every waking moment, every expenditure of energy: God cares about what you do. And the bar is set very high. I must be holy; I must love my enemies. Read Matthew 5: You haven't murdered anybody? Good; but if you have harbored anger in your heart you are guilty. Haven't committed adultery? Good; but if you have lust in your heart you are guilty.

This is not a counsel of despair! This is our hope. Otherwise we live animalistic lives, and nothing really matters. To believe in Christ as the judge is to recognize that "cheap grace is grace without discipleship, grace without the cross, grace without Jesus Christ. Such grace is costly because it calls us to follow, and it is grace because it calls us to follow Jesus Christ. It is costly because it costs a man his life, and it is grace because it gives a man the only true life" (Dietrich Bonhoeffer).[2] Judgment is creative for those who "get it." Judgment is all love, not an inquisition or a gulag. Jesus comes "from thence," not from despotic, vengeful rage, but from the Father Almighty's love.

And the inner secret of a life eager to be attached to Christ as our judge is this: God's judgment on our sinfulness falls on Jesus, God's own son. He is "the Judge judged in our place" (Karl Barth).[3] On the cross, Jesus' heart was broken, literally bursting with love for us, taking into itself all of our waywardness, our superficiality, our smugness, our revolt, praying not just for Roman soldiers but for us: "Father, forgive them, for they know not what they do." Thanks be to God that, over days, weeks, years, we may come to know what we do. And the knowledge of what we do, the cleansing bath of Christ's love, the refining fire of God's Spirit are our hope, our comfort, our challenge.

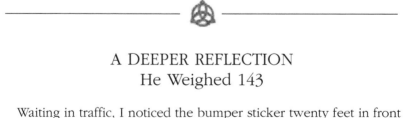

A DEEPER REFLECTION
He Weighed 143

Waiting in traffic, I noticed the bumper sticker twenty feet in front of me: "Christ is coming again soon. Look busy." Busy doing good,

I assume, not busy doing, well, other things. "From thence he shall come to judge the quick and the dead." At the very beginning of Arthur Miller's play *After the Fall,* the stage is entirely barren except for a lone metal chair center stage. Quentin, an attorney, walks on stage. Or we should say "ex-attorney"; he has just forsaken the practice of law. He finds no meaning in life, so why bother with the law? His monologue meanders to this confession: "I've quit the firm. I couldn't concentrate any more. I felt I was merely in the service of my own success. It all lost any point. I looked up one day and the bench was empty. No judge in sight. And all that remained was the endless argument with myself. A pointless litigation with existence before an empty bench, which, of course, is another way of saying despair."[4]

An empty bench, no judge in sight. Then the clergy, the one other profession that wears flowing robes, insist the bench is not empty; the judge is not exactly in sight; he was here, and he'll be back in a moment. I have a theologically cynical friend who finds the notion of God-as-judge unappetizing, unpleasant. But I counter by saying we had better hope there is a judge who'll occupy the bench, because if there is no such thing as judgment, then the terrorists, child abusers, thieves, and swindlers get away with it, and there will never be a reckoning. We pray for the reckoning, for judgment.

Them versus Us

You may be fond of the way this sermon has commenced, zealous as we may be for God's judgment upon the terrorists, child abusers, thieves, and swindlers. But the Creed does not say, "From thence he shall come to judge those terrible people out there," but "the quick and the dead." Virtually all of us are quick (perhaps an overflattering term), and so the object of Jesus' judgment would be not them, but us, not just you, but me. He will judge everyone, from Adolf Hitler to Mother Teresa, from Osama bin Laden to Francis of Assisi. And judgment does not merely happen in a single lightning stroke at the end of time; judgment happens every week, every day, every moment. Now. And also now. God is relentlessly nosy. God is inside your head and knows every thought that passes through your cranium, every bad attitude you harbor, every speck of ugliness in you, what you do when no one is looking, mental conjurings you dare not admit even to yourself. And God is not pleased by much of what goes on. God is not pleased by some thoughts and actions that you actually like, and may even feel are highly moral. Your standard of measure is illegible in the shadow of God's standard.

During my first week as a pastor, somebody called on Thursday to tell me I would be teaching Sunday School and the lesson would be the Ten Commandments. I hoisted a dozen books on Exodus and Israelite religion out of my boxes and prepared a sterling lecture. But it never happened. I met my class, a school guidance counselor read the Ten Commandments out loud, and then a brickmason raised his hand and announced, "I have never violated any of these." I wanted to love and be loved by these people sitting before me, so I was pained to try to explain how they, how we together, are in fact frequent and habitual violators of all Ten Commandments. In the years since then, my members have included a real-life murderer, a sizable batch of adulterers, and a veritable legion of coveters. But without ever having met my new class, I knew we had murderers, adulterers, coveters, Sabbath nonobservers, not to mention idolaters—good people I love to this day. But they (truly, we) "have sinned and fallen short of the glory of God." And it's Jesus' fault, isn't it? Whatever wiggle room we might otherwise be able to negotiate is shut down in the Sermon on the Mount. Haven't murdered? But have you been angry? Haven't committed adultery? But have you lusted? Coveting: the engine of capitalism. John Calvin said the human mind is a continuously running factory of idols.

The Bar Is High

What chance do we have? The bar is too high. But isn't this the nobility of humanity, the hope of our lives, that God does not set the bar low so you can waddle over it with no effort? And isn't this the modesty of faith, for the bar is so high that even the most nimble-souled super-Christian cannot jump up, grab on, and smile down self-righteously on the rest of us? We see the bar, and we leap up, gritting our teeth, doing our best. We stumble and fall, but we leap again, a little better than last time, but still woefully short. We pray, "Forgive me, empower me," and God does. We leap, a smidgeon higher, and noticeably closer to the bar. But just when it's barely eluding our grasp, the bar seems to drift, higher, further, and we are that much short again. "Forgive me, empower me," and God does. We leap, a smidgeon higher, and noticeably closer to the bar. But just when it's barely eluding our grasp, it seems to drift higher. This is God's way of binding us to God's own heart. God shields us from complacency, from smugness. The more we plumb the depths of the heart of God, the more we know we are not God, but then at the same time we inch closer to God. This is the grace of judgment.

During the season of Lent, we are more attentive than usual to God's nosiness, focusing on the fact that God is inside my head, God is inside my body; God cares what I put into my body, where I take my body, and what I do with it. Some people say, "Don't give up something for Lent; take something on!" But haven't we already taken on so much that there is no room in the inn, no time or space to let God do the radical surgery required on the soul? Some people say, "Giving up something like chocolate for Lent is just so trivial." I've given up chocolate for Lent many times, and the mere triviality of this exercise exposes how trivial my soul has become. It's only chocolate, but I adore it so, and not having chocolate can send my head into a tailspin. And then I realize how easily I am thrown off balance, how Jesus is not yet my Lord, how so many of our Lord's children on this planet can never get what I deny myself for a season. And I recognize underneath my craving the one delight I genuinely crave, and that is the presence of Jesus.

A friend asked the other day what he might give up for Lent. "Knowing you," I said, "you might give up golf." "Golf? I could never give up golf for forty days." "Then that's your answer." Golf is nothing in itself, and golf is different from chocolate, in that eating chocolate takes only a delicious minute, whereas golf devours three or four hours. "Take your golf time and talk to your wife. Pray (which you tell me you don't have time to do). Read your Bible, volunteer at the homeless shelter. Just for a season. And see if your faith takes any new tangibility." Realizing we stand before an occupied bench, we say, "Lord, there is nothing I'm going to hold on to that will prevent me from becoming the person that you want me to be."

Subjecting ourselves to God's judgment is not a negative, it is not a sacrifice; God does not come, switch in hand, to give us a whipping. The judge is the one who loves, who was born of the virgin Mary, suffered under Pontius Pilate, was crucified, dead and buried;

he descended into hell; on the third day he rose from the dead, and ascended into heaven. The judge is in sight, and he is our hope; yielding to his judgment is the most selfish thing we could ever do. God is yearning, inviting us to draw near to his heart, so we might not squander our lives in two-bit living, so we might be who God made us to be.

To Spread Grace Around

Sometimes, we learn about judgment not by cowering in fear, but by taking a long look at someone who is genuinely good. The person I have chosen today is Mister Rogers. I can't say I was a huge fan of Mister Rogers; my kids preferred *Sesame Street*. But in the wake of his death, I read a wonderful article by a journalist named Tom Junod[5] who followed Mister Rogers around for a while and told about his remarkable mission to spread grace around the world. Do you know how much Mister Rogers weighed? Thirty-three years ago Fred Rogers stepped on a scale, and he weighed 143, and he still weighed 143 when he died—a number he thought of as a gift, a destiny fulfilled. He said, "The number 143 means I love you. You get it? It takes one letter to say 'I,' four to say 'love' and three to say 'you.' 143 means I love you. Isn't that wonderful?" Parenthetically, I stepped on the scales yesterday and looked down; I think what the scale said to me was "I worried today."

Fred Rogers went to seminary, but then TV was invented and he watched TV. He watched people throwing pies into each other's faces on TV, and this made him sad. It made him want to take TV on and do some good, to spread some grace. So about a thousand times he took off his jacket and shoes and put on a sweater and sneakers and turned out Mister Rogers's neighborhood. How big was his show?

One boy, who was born with an acute case of cerebral palsy, was treated terribly as a young child, and then he went to another home where his mother noticed how he watched *Mister Rogers' Neighborhood*. She believed Mister Rogers was keeping her son alive. Some big foundation worked it out for Mister Rogers to visit this boy, and when he did, Mister Rogers asked, "Would you pray for me?" The boy was thunderstruck because nobody had ever asked him for anything. He was the object of prayer, not the one to pray for Mister Rogers. But now he prays for Mister Rogers and he doesn't want to die anymore. Tom Junod witnessed this and privately he congratulated Mister Rogers for being so smart. But Mister Rogers didn't know what he meant. He really wanted the boy's prayers, saying, "I think that anyone who's gone through challenges like that must be very close to God."

Another boy suffered from autism, and in fact, the boy never spoke, ever, until one day he said, "X the owl," which is the name of one of Mister Rogers's puppets. The boy had never looked his father in the eye until one day his father said, "Let's go to Mister Rogers's neighborhood." And they went all the way from Boise, Idaho. And Mister Rogers played with the boy who now is speaking and reading.

Mister Rogers got a lifetime Emmy award, and here are Tom Junod's exact words to describe the scene,

> There, in front of the stars, in front of all the jutting jaws and salt-water bosoms, he made a small bow and said, "All of us have special ones who have loved us into being. Would you just take, along with me, ten seconds to think of the people who have helped you become who you are. . . . Ten seconds of silence." Then he lifted his wrist, looked at the audience, and looked at his watch, and said softly, "I'll watch the time," and there was, at first, a small whoop from the crowd, a giddy hiccup of laughter as people realized he wasn't kidding, that Mister Rogers was not some convenient eunuch but rather a man, an authority figure who actually expected them to do what he asked . . . and so they did. One second, two seconds, three. . . . and now the jaws clenched, the bosoms heaved, the mascara ran, the tears fell upon the beglittered gathering like rain leaking down a crystal chandelier, and Mister Rogers finally looked up from his watch and said, "May God be with you" to all his vanquished children.

Another boy without such obvious problems ran up to Mister Rogers, yelling and waving a big plastic sword. Mister Rogers bent over, whispered in the boy's ear, and the boy put the sword away, smiled, and hugged Mister Rogers. Tom Junod, the journalist, asked what he said, and Mister Rogers said, "Oh, I just told him he really didn't need that sword to be strong on the outside, because he's very strong on the inside."

You Were a Child Once

A big group of ophthalmologists came to Mister Rogers hoping he'd produce something for children so they wouldn't be so afraid to go to the eye doctor. What Mister Rogers did was this: On a big piece of paper, he wrote, "Remember you were a child once, too," and handed it to them.

Ever since I read all this, and much more about Mister Rogers, I am really missing him, and I keep thinking about life and peace and people, and it seems to me that it's all really very simple. You were a child once, too. We exist for one very simple purpose. To spread grace around. Play with somebody. Encourage somebody. Ask somebody to pray for you. Remember who helped you. Listen to your body's messages. Be gentle. Smile. And make the most of this beautiful day. It's such a good feeling to know we're friends. It's a beautiful day in the neighborhood.

If this reverie about Mister Rogers hasn't clicked in with you who came today wondering about Christ coming to judge the quick and the dead, let me add what the journalist Junod wrote in a eulogy for *Esquire* after Mister Rogers left the quick and joined the dead:

> He was not only the kindest man I'd ever met, but also one of the most fiercely disciplined, to the degree that he saw nothing but the good in other human beings. When he saw the good in me, he fixed on it, and there was never a moment in which he didn't try to make me live up to it, by word, or by example, or most often, by prayer.[6]

And Mister Rogers prayed from 5:00 until 7:00 every morning for people like Tom Junod, ophthalmologists, a boy with a sword, television stars, a boy with autism, and another with cerebral palsy. Jesus—the one who is coming to judge the quick and the dead—also sees and fixes on the good in us, and tries by word and example to make us live up to it. And Jesus prays, not only for those shadowy hours when darkness is dispelled by the dawn, but all the time.

You were a child once, and you still are. And when you're a child, you look up to your father. And what you really want to do is to please him because you know that he loves you. Arthur Miller's Quentin, by the way, offers another more hopeful musing:

With all this darkness, the truth is that every morning when I awake, I'm full of hope! I'm like a boy again. For an instant, there's some unformed promise in the air. I jump out of bed, can't wait to finish breakfast—but then it seeps into my room, my life and its pointlessness. I thought—if I could corner that hope, find what it consists of and either kill it for a lie, or really make it mine.[7]

An unformed promise. The judge will be back in a moment. Jump out of bed, corner that hope, and leap for the bar.

Notes

1. For reflections on these words, see James C. Howell, *Yours Are the Hands of Christ: The Practice of Faith* (Nashville: Upper Room, 1999).

2. Dietrich Bonhoeffer, *The Cost of Discipleship*, rev. ed., trans. R. H. Fuller (New York: Macmillan, 1963), 47.

3. Karl Barth, *Church Dogmatics* IV.1 (Edinburgh: T.&T. Clark, 1956), 211ff.

4. Arthur Miller, *After the Fall: A Play in Two Acts* (New York: Penguin, 1964), 3.

5. Tom Junod, "Can You Say . . . Hero?" *Esquire*, November 1998; reprinted in *Best Spiritual Writing 1999*, ed. Philip Zaleski and Kathleen Norris (New York: HarperCollins, 1999).

6. "Remembering Mister Rogers," *Esquire*, March 2003.

7. Miller, *After the Fall*, 3-4.

Chapter Ten

THE HOLY SPIRIT

LESSON 24
I BELIEVE IN THE HOLY SPIRIT (PART 1)

*The Holy Spirit will teach you all things, reminding you
of all I have said. (John 14:26, AP)*

hat (or who) is the Holy Spirit? Frederick Dale Bruner called the Holy Spirit the "shy member" of the Trinity.[1] The Spirit is everywhere and active, but not always right out in the open. We don't have paintings of the Spirit. The Hebrew word for "spirit," *ruach,* means "breath" or "wind." The Spirit is personal, very personal, as personal as your next breath, and yet as elusive as the wind, as invisible as the wind, yet powerful, with noticeable effects.

When God created everything, "the Spirit of God was moving over the waters" (Genesis 1:2). Too often we think of the Holy Spirit as involved in the inner, pious life, forgetting that the Spirit is "the breath of life which causes all creation, all history, to flow together to its ultimate end, in the infinite ocean of God," as Pope John Paul II so beautifully described it. I love this poem written by Hildegard of Bingen:

The Holy Spirit is life-giving life,
Universal Mover and the root of all creation,

refiner of all things from their dross,
brings forgiveness of guilt and oil for our wounds,
is radiance of life, most worthy of worship,
wakening and reawakening both earth and heaven.[2]

When Jesus was baptized in the Jordan, God the Father was over-heard speaking from heaven, saying, "This is my beloved Son." Then at that moment, the Spirit descended on him, like a dove (Matthew 3:13). Jesus is driven, motivated by the Spirit; Jesus relies on the Spirit at every turn. And just as he is about to die, Jesus encourages the forlorn disciples by promising to send the Spirit once he has gone (see John 15:26, 16:7); Jesus leaves, but the disciples get the Spirit, who comforts them, who teaches them what is true and what isn't, who moves them to continue to follow Jesus. The Spirit is "shy," self-effacing. The Spirit draws attention, not to the Spirit, but to God the Father, to Jesus. We could say that the Spirit makes Jesus real to us.

The Spirit's vehicle is the Bible, which we think of as "inspired"—meaning "breathed in." The Holy Spirit, the living breath of God, breathed into these stories, poems, and letters the life of God, so that the Bible might live with us, so that we might grasp the universe from God's perspective, so that we might read, and understand, what living with and for God is all about. So "inspiration" isn't some radioactive property emanating from the Bible. Rather, "inspiration" is how God *uses* this book in our lives. "All scripture is inspired by God, and profitable for teaching, for reproof, for correction, and for training in righteousness, that [you] may be complete, equipped for every good work" (2 Timothy 3:16-17). If you imagine the Bible as inspired, then expect to be educated, reprimanded, disciplined, readied by the Spirit to charge out and do good in the world.

Over the next two lessons, we will talk about the Holy Spirit and you; and about what the Holy Spirit does in the Church and in the world, reflecting on Evelyn Underhill's wise words: "There is no place or cranny where He is not; no situation in which He is not interested and in which He does not act—none therefore to which we can refuse interest, or in which we can dare to do less than our best."[3]

LESSON 25
I BELIEVE IN THE HOLY SPIRIT (PART 2)

The spirit of the LORD will possess you, and you will be turned into a different person. (1 Samuel 10:6, AP)

Fairly often, I talk with someone giving up on God because "I just don't feel what I think I am supposed to feel." I guess I feel sad that feelings have become the litmus test of whether the Spirit is a reality. Relationships and life are more than feelings. The Holy Spirit is with you and me always, whether we feel it or know it or not. Martin Luther worried that a tumult of spiritual feeling can actually be the work of the devil, who hopes that we will give up on God once we find ourselves in a dry, barren desert of emotion. "Feelings are the chocolate creams of the Christian life. It is by no means always the perfect lovers who have such feelings. Do not make the mistake of thinking, if you sometimes feel cold and dead, that you do not know how to love" (Evelyn Underhill).[4]

You may have had profound, wonderful feelings about God, but the Holy Spirit is far larger than your feelings. Listen to Oscar Romero: "God is not failing us when we don't feel his presence. God exists, and he exists even more, the farther you feel from him. When you feel the anguished desire for God to come near because you don't feel him present, then God is very close to your anguish. God is always our Father and never forsakes us, and that we are closer to him than we think."[5]

The Holy Spirit may (and will!) be the catalyst for startling changes in your life. Jesus came into the world, not so we might *feel* different, but so we could *be* different. The Holy Spirit will nurture a whole new set of attitudes, will be the spark to ignite an unforeseen passion for God. The Holy Spirit will stir your heart to obey God, to be holy, to be assured of God's unfailing presence. The Holy Spirit will actually wrap up our feelings in the Spirit's loving embrace, for some of what we feel needs some healing.

"Likewise the Spirit helps us in our weakness. For we do not know how to pray as we ought, but the Spirit himself intercedes for us with sighs too deep for words. . . . He who searches [our hearts] knows what is the mind of the Spirit, because the Spirit intercedes for the saints according to the will of God" (Romans 8:26-27). Saint Basil wrote quite hopefully, "Through the Spirit we become intimate with God."[6] "God sent the Spirit of his Son into our hearts, crying, 'Abba! Father!'" (Galatians 4:6). "When we cry, 'Abba! Father!' it is the Spirit bearing witness with our spirit that we are children of God, and if children then heirs of God, provided we suffer with him in order that we may also be glorified with him" (Romans 8:16-17). The Spirit is the bridge into a close relationship with God.

This thought is not entirely comfortable. The Spirit "searches everything" (1 Corinthians 2:10), and we may wish the Spirit were not quite so nosy. Theologians speak of "sanctification." "Justification" (our salvation) is what God has done *for* us. "Sanctification" (meaning "made holy") is what God does *in* us. You aren't saved just so you can get into heaven; you are saved to be transformed, changed into a different person, or, rather, into the true person you were made to be. The Spirit makes you holy.

Holiness is not a matter of gritting your teeth and trying really diligently to do what God requires. We may grit our teeth, and we do try hard. But I am not able to do what God wants of me, I am not capable of the life God wants for me. A changed life is the gift of God's Spirit. As a humble believer, I know that any good that I manage is "not I, but Christ in me" (Galatians 2:20, AP). Paul described this new life, the life for which we were made, the only life that will ever satisfy us, as "the fruit of the Spirit." Not "the fruit of my good intentions," but "the fruit of the Spirit": "love, joy, peace, patience, kindness, goodness, faithfulness, gentleness, self-control; against such there is no law" (Galatians 5:22-23).

LESSON 26
I BELIEVE IN THE HOLY SPIRIT (PART 3)

When the day of Pentecost had come, they were all filled with the Holy Spirit . . . and began to speak in other tongues. (Acts 2:1-4)

In the Bible, the Holy Spirit certainly works one on one with individuals, but the Spirit's all-enveloping desire is to bring each person into relationship with others, almost like the square dance caller urging people off the sidelines into the circle, moving, listening to the next direction, joining hands, circling, smiling, delighting in the dance; and that space in the middle of the circle around which we move together is Christ, whose presence is palpable in the actions of the dancers.

We say the Church was "born" at Pentecost (Acts 2), when the Spirit caught everyone by surprise, rifling through the upper room like wind, or fire, some tornado of white hot heat. The Church's first moment of existence was not a still life, pastel figures posing serenely in prayer; instead, there was rushing, people flying out of the exits, speaking words they hadn't known five minutes before, bent on grabbing the next person in the marketplace and hugging them with a transforming word about Jesus.

Nothing is more essential in the life of the Church than for the Church to develop a keen awareness of what the Spirit is doing in the Church, and with the Church. Worship is not a concert or speech we observe; worship, if we listen closely, is the movement of the Spirit, detectable in a head bowed, the rustling of bulletins, pregnant silences, a soaring descant, truth spoken—and even in the announcements. "Pray for Alice Bolton" or "BBQ on sale for youth missions" are not just nice ideas, but the Spirit directing the dance.

Annie Dillard said that if we consider the potential for the eruption of the Spirit in worship, we ought to wear crash helmets out in the pews.[7] The Spirit most certainly is a great comfort, a holy solace to us; and yet the Spirit inevitably catapults us out of the building and into mission. The New Testament's Greek word for Church is *ekklesia*, which means "called out." We are called out of the dance, out of the hall, to grab the hand of somebody who is hurting, lonely, poor, hollow. The Church is not a club, a nice place where nice people do nice things with other nice people. We "speak in tongues"—meaning we find the language to tell our story to people who don't speak our language.

And I don't mean English! I mean church-talk. More and more people out there have never been in church, do not know what Sunday School or a board is, do not own a Bible—and we are called to find the words, to meet people where they are and share the tantalizing, life-changing story of the Gospel. Inviting someone to church, living differently, being good without getting smug—you never know how you might connect with someone, and before you know it he's with us in a do-si-do, or she's with us in an alaman-left, those fascinating movements of the Spirit's *ekklesia*.

For now, we should notice that many churches are analyzing carefully how they are structured, how they do business, what they really are all about; and most of this is helpful, shifting the whole mental approach closer to what God is calling the Church to be. Churches long to be led, not just by smart, careful people, but by the Holy Spirit, who will "move us to dare great things for God."[8]

A DEEPER REFLECTION
The Shy Member

I keep thinking about the wisdom (and I hope it's not utter nonsense) of the theologian who said, "The Holy Spirit is the shy member of the Trinity." Bracketing for the moment questions we may have about the Trinity, if the Holy Spirit is God, how could God get away with being shy for even a minute? Many Christians are anything but shy when it comes to the Holy Spirit. You may know such spiritually confident Christians, who seem to be on familiar terms with the Spirit, as if that Spirit is in the next room, and they had a lovely visit together just a few moments ago, exchanging words and affection. Then there are others for whom the Spirit is never mentioned, so baffling, confusing, or perhaps unreal is this undoubtedly shy member of the Trinity. They peek under rugs, they look behind doors, they stare into the mirror or their navels, and see nothing.

When I consider these two groups of people, I wonder if it was God's design that they would make each other miserable. Or better, if it were God's design that they might learn to talk to each other, and somehow together discern the truth about the Holy Spirit, which is neither entirely obvious, yet is not entirely mystifying either. Shy people do not insist on their own way, they let others shine for a while; typically they listen attentively; when they step forward, they surprise you every time. So were the Spirit shy, we might let this shyness help us stand back and listen, learn, and be surprised.

Where Is the Holy Spirit?

When I had been a pastor for just over one month, with a face that could still pass for that of a teenager, I heard a knock at the door of my parsonage, with its unfortunate location in the same yard as the church building. "Is that the Methodist church?" a grinning stranger asked. I said yes. "Is this the parsonage?" "Yes ma'am, it is." "Well, I need to speak to the minister. Is your father at home?" *Just say no,* I told myself. She proceeded to press me to advertise an event in a nearby village: "It's going to be so exciting. The Holy Spirit is going to be there. I want your people to come at 11 on Sunday." I said, "But we have worship at 11!" "Oh, this is different. The Holy Spirit will *really* be over there with us."

Is the Holy Spirit in one place and not another place? How would we measure anyhow? By a rush of emotion? Doesn't the Spirit frequent places where there is no feeling, where feelings have grown cold, where the predominant mood is sorrow? Or hollowness? Or solid consistency? If we associate the Spirit with feeling, don't we merely mirror what dominates everything else in our society? A marriage falters—because "I don't feel what I once felt for her. I need what I felt on our honeymoon eighteen years ago." The issue of gay marriage: isn't the deeper confusion that, for homosexuals or heterosexuals, when we ask about marriage, we are not coming to the church, in effect asking God for permission to live together, to sanctify a commitment? Instead, people have been acting on their feelings for quite some time and are talking about nothing more than legalities. Isn't our ethic "If it feels good, it must be good"? Many things that feel good that are not good; and so much that is so good does not feel good at all. The Holy Spirit is about goodness, commitment, holiness. The Holy Spirit comes not to indulge our emotions. The Holy Spirit comes to change us, to transform us, to make us holy, to make us into the people that God created us to be.

But do not misunderstand. Only the dominant zone of my brain deduces that this woman who appeared at my door was wrongheaded. In some other region of my brain, or maybe in my gut someplace, I have this hunch that she was on to something, that she had been seized by something so strong that she forgot how to be polite; and however much I value decorum, something deep inside me yearns to be swept up and aloft by something bigger than myself. If there is a Spirit, shouldn't there be at least an occasional, soaring moment of ecstasy, when I am "lost in wonder, love, and praise"? If there is a Spirit, does sitting rigidly in a pew with a sour face make sense? If the Spirit isn't an emotion, might the Spirit not be keenly interested in my emotions, in that "zoo of lusts, a bedlam of ambitions, a nursery of fears, a harem of fondled hatreds," as C. S. Lewis described,[9] and might I not find my submerged, inner life jumped unexpectedly by this Spirit? And before I know it, might I feel at least something, or might my crazed jumble of emotions experience a bit of healing?

The Bible's words for Spirit signify air that is moving. So the Spirit's work is noticed in all sorts of diverse places, although the shy Spirit slinks behind a rock so you notice the work instead of the worker. The breath you took—just now—is the Spirit lovingly giving you life. The wind rustles through the leaves: the Spirit laughing through autumn. You discern some pattern in the clouds, refracting the light into reddish hues: every instance of beauty is a masterpiece of the Spirit, whose signature on the art is visible only as beauty itself. You hear the soaring descant of the soprano that breaks your heart or the smile on a child's face. We see the Spirit's work all the time, but not the Spirit itself, that shy member of the Trinity. It's not a matter of what we see, but how we see what we see.

The Holy Spirit comes so we might have a relationship with God. The Holy Spirit comes so Jesus Christ can be lifted off the pages of history, no longer a relic in the museum of our religious past. This Jesus is God's precious gift to us, and the Spirit is the giver, the singing telegram, the package deliverer who brings the gift to the door but seems to dash off before we see who left the wonder. And when Jesus is present, we are different, we become good (or at least better), we live boldly, we are healed, we join hands with others and dance a jig or two.

Discerning the Spirit

The shy Spirit's constant labor engages us in the simplest, most mundane moments. We ask, "Should I do this or that? Do I go here or there? Do I spend on this or that or nothing?" This enormously important exercise, this training in virtue, can be frustrating. We wish the Spirit were a bit less shy, but then the Spirit wants us, bumbling toddlers that we are, to learn to stand on our own feet and walk. Perhaps the gravest cause of our frustration in being led by the Spirit involves time. We put in so little time with God, it's little wonder we have such a poorly developed relationship. "God, I prayed for fifteen seconds three days ago. Why haven't you fixed everything yet? I did have a minute and a half quickie devotional on Monday! Why hasn't the week gone better than it has?"

As a boy, J. R. R. Tolkien loved trees, talked with them, and could not bear to see one cut down. In *The Lord of the Rings*, he created talking tree-like creatures called Ents. They speak a peculiar language called Entish—and these speakers of Entish talk so ploddingly that patience must be mustered to listen. As Tolkien puts it, "Entish is a lovely language, but it takes a very long time to say anything in Entish, because we do not say anything in Entish unless it is worth taking a very long time to say it, or to listen to it."[10] The Hobbits are like us, frantically urging the Ents, "Come on, get it out, hurry up, move on!" But this shy Spirit does not rush in and talk rapidly or loudly. The shy voice is barely a whisper and is slow, taking time to say what is worth saying, and we have no choice but to put in the time, and the quiet, if we have the slightest interest in what the Spirit might have to say.

To keep us humble, this shy Spirit even wired reality because we are seeking God's will doesn't mean we will in fact know or do God's will. Fallacies pollute our discernment, such as the fallacy of the open door. People say, "The door was open, so it was of God." But plenty of open doors should not be walked through at all! And some doors God would call us to are locked shut, and if we follow we have to bang, push, kick, and crowbar the things open.

The Spirit in the Church

Pushing open the doors of the church itself can be difficult, as we unwittingly have installed deadbolts that keep the Spirit out—or tried to. The Spirit can never be shut out, thank goodness, and the shy Spirit occasionally overcomes her shyness and invades our space like some tornado, cleaning house, ushering in new life. My first church, the one with the parsonage in the yard, had a festive covered-dish dinner at Thanksgiving each year. Only the bedridden ever missed it; all eighty members in attendance, the women brandishing their finest casseroles and pies. An after-dinner tradition had developed: one of the women, a guidance counselor at the county school, would target some family in need, and when the dinner was ended, the ladies would package up a huge box of sumptuous food for delivery to the needy.

I floated back to thank these culinary wizards when the Spirit blew into the kitchen uninvited. One of the saints, a bit weary at the end of a long day, declared she was tired, and in an annoyed voice wondered out loud why on earth she had to go and take this food to somebody she didn't even know. Shaking her head in the chagrin of self-pity, she muttered, "Why do we have to deliver this food late like this? I don't understand why in the world we take food to somebody who could have come here themselves two hours ago and have eaten it already."

Glances were exchanged, heads were cocked, and a conversation commenced. Why *do* we deliver food when the family could have come and eaten it with us? So somebody tossed out the delicious idea that next year the guidance counselor would find a family and we'd just invite them to come. As shy as the Spirit, Janice Woodring did come, with her two boys, a little tentative at first, but then everyone was so welcoming, the food so tasty. The women still packaged up extra food to send home, and someone asked if they could pick them up on the way to church Sunday morning. Janice asked, "What is the dress code?" and the quickest-thinking church member I have ever known answered, "Whatever you have on." So they came.

And they came back. Somebody started tutoring the boys and bought them some shoes. Somebody else helped Janice find a job and get her budget in order. She volunteered to help keep the nursery, she loved children so much. Then she helped out a desperate elementary teacher with Sunday School one morning and stayed a year. One day Janice rang my doorbell and nervously mumbled that she wondered if she and her boys could join our Church. I said, "We'd be so delighted to have you; we'll do it this Sunday." Her head lowered a little, and she said, "But I don't really have anything to offer to this Church." I said, "You have given us so much, more than you could ever imagine." She gave us a noble privilege: for if someone should say, "I have never heard of the Holy Spirit," we now can say, "We had heard of him with our ears, but now our eyes have seen him" (Job 42:5, AP).

Notes

1. Frederick Dale Bruner, *The Holy Spirit—Shy Member of the Trinity* (Philadelphia: Augsburg, 1984). Vladimir Lossky, *The Mystical Theology of the Eastern Church* (Crestwood, N.Y.: St. Vladimir's Seminary Press, 2002), 160f, teaches us that in the Eastern Orthodox tradition, the Holy Spirit "remains unmanifested, hidden, concealing Himself in His very appearing. . . . The doctrine of the Holy Spirit (in contrast to the dazzling manifestation of the Son which the Church proclaims to the farthest confines of the universe) has the character of a secret."

2. Hildegard of Bingen, *Mystical Writings*, ed. Fiona Bowie and Oliver Davies (New York: Crossroad, 1990), 118.

3. Evelyn Underhill, *The School of Charity: Meditations on the Christian Creed* (Harrisburg, Pa.: Morehouse Publishing, 1991), 78.

4. Evelyn Underhill, *The Ways of the Spirit*, ed. Grace Adolphsen Brame (New York: Crossroad, 1996), 62.

5. Oscar Romero, *The Violence of Love*, trans. James R. Brockman (Farmington, Pa.: Plough Publishing House, 1988), 131.

6. Saint Basil, *On the Holy Spirit* (Crestwood, N. Y.: St. Vladimir's Seminary Press, 2001), 77.

7. Annie Dillard, *Teaching a Stone to Talk: Expeditions and Encounters* (New York: HarperPerennial, 1982), 58: "On the whole, I do not find Christians sufficiently sensible of conditions. Does anyone have the foggiest idea what sort of power we so blithely invoke? Or, as I suspect, does no one believe a word of it? The churches are children playing on the floor with their chemistry sets, mixing up a batch of TNT to kill a Sunday morning. It is madness to wear ladies' straw hats and velvet hats to church; we should all be wearing crash helmets. Ushers should issue life preservers and signal flares; they should lash us to our pews. For the sleeping god may wake someday and take offense."

8. The phrase comes from one of many great books on changing Church culture from "what we want to do," "what suits us," to "what God wants us to do" (Anthony B. Robinson, *Transforming Congregational Culture* [Grand Rapids: Eerdmans, 2003], 102).

9. C. S. Lewis, *Surprised by Joy* (New York: Harvest, 1970), 226.

10. J. R. R. Tolkien, *The Two Towers* (New York: Ballantine, 1965), 80.

Chapter   Eleven

THE HOLY CATHOLIC CHURCH

LESSON 27
CATHOLIC CHURCH

*Now there are varieties of gifts, but the same Spirit;
and there are varieties of service, but the same Lord; and
there are varieties of working, but it is the same God who
inspires them all in every one. (1 Corinthians 12:4-6)*

I am unsure which of these three words should have the largest question mark attached to it. Catholic? Holy? Church? By "catholic," the Creed does not mean the denomination, the Roman Catholic Church. The adjective "catholic" (with a little c) means something like complete, whole, united. But churches are far from united! We compete with the Presbyterians for new members. Southern Baptists tell us our Baptism isn't really Baptism at all; the Episcopalians are battling among themselves on the issue of homosexuality; blacks and whites keep themselves segregated, as do the rich and poor; and our Catholic friends continue to take it on the chin for past misdeeds. God must look down and weep at the sibling rivalry, the mindless division in the Church for which Christ gave his life.

Or does God grin a little? Does God have designs on how to use even our fractured churches? Clearly Christians don't have their act together, but God exploits our inability, turning our shattered unity into a curious collection of broken windows, through which different kinds of broken people still manage to climb into the kingdom of God. The Baptists know the centrality of the Bible. The Quakers embrace the need for silence. Methodists try to engage social issues. The Catholics embody the rich tradition of the faith and the need for saints. The nondenominational denominations creatively reach people wary of churchiness. Mennonites are humble, Presbyterians use their brains, and the AME Zions can outsing us all. We mainliners who are stiffly fixed in our pews need a little liberation from the Pentecostals so we, too, can show a little emotion and move, if only a little bit. The evangelicals want to save souls, while some of the more "liberal" groups want to administer medicine and food. Surely both are needed. Independent congregations can teach us all to take initiative, while connectional churches with bishops and even a pope can expand our vision and realize we are part of something bigger, that we in fact have in common the only thing that really matters: Jesus Christ. Faith can see beyond the divisions, the differences. We really are one Church (at least we are to God), going in every way conceivable after our real competition, which is never another church, but rather that many-headed monster of cynicism, hollowness, violence, greed, hedonism, selfishness, and disbelief.

So, "I believe in the 'catholic' Church" is a prayer, a longing, a searching after our elusive unity in Christ, a reminder that we all get it wrong, and at times we get it right, and we anticipate life with God in heaven, where there will be no "sections" for various denominational bodies. When I worship in my Church, I am mystically joined with Christians across the street—and across the ocean—in every place and language on God's earth. John Wesley's advice is helpful:

> Let us keep close to the grand scriptural doctrines everywhere delivered. There are many doctrines of a less essential nature, with regard to which even sincere children of God (due to the weakness of human understanding) are divided. In these, we may think and let think. We may agree to disagree. But let us hold fast the essentials of the faith once delivered to the saints, strongly insisted on at all times and in all places.[1]

116

LESSON 28
HOLY CHURCH

They devoted themselves to teaching, to fellowship, to breaking bread, and to praying. Their hearts were glad and generous, praising God; and the Lord added to their number those being saved. (Acts 2:42, 46-47, AP)

Religious life in America today has become a private affair. There is a dogged individualism about our faith, even among churchgoers. Increasing numbers of people feel they can be Christian without bothering with Church. But how lonely, how sad! Faith is something we do together, something that presses us up against people with whom we normally might have no contact at all, only to discover that with regard to what really matters, we are brothers and sisters in God's quirky family. I am saved to be saved with you, us together. We desperately need to connect with others at a deep, faith level. "God has and will continue to give us company so that we will know how rightly to worship . . . to make our faithful living possible through that skill called memory" (Stanley Hauerwas).[2]

Saint Augustine said that to love another person is to help that person to love God.[3] How unlikely that my private ruminations, my inner stirrings, could actually prove to be "the truth" about God. To grow beyond my pet biases, I need the give-and-take we can enjoy in the Church. We test our beliefs, exposing ourselves to the insights—and doubts!—of others. We let the Church scrutinize our lives. Where else can you be talked to about life and death? Where else will you go to be reminded that you are not just a bundle of desires, that you are more than a worker for some company's profit margin, that you have a spiritual side? Where else will you hear any word even subtly challenging our culture? And how will you make a difference in the world?[4]

The Church, for all its foibles and triviality, is our best hope of reaching upward and outward toward God and those in need. The Church is not holy; the Church can be an embarrassing caricature of itself. We pray to be transformed into a "holy Church." And yet, perhaps it is the Church's foolishness that stands as the open door to

117

people who are not perfect either, who do not have everything all figured out—an open door so we can be the kind of crowd John Wesley envisioned back in 1743 at the beginnings of Methodism, "a company of men having the form and seeking the power of godliness, united in order to pray together, to receive the word of exhortation, and to watch over one another in love, that they may help each other to work out their salvation."[5]

Watching over one another in love, praying together, and serving together. Paul imagined the Church as the "Body of Christ," different members, but joined in a single unit, with various abilities, passions, gifts, weaknesses. This is our stupendous assignment, our precious privilege. Together we may pray these words from Lancelot Andrewes:

> Lord Jesus, I give you my hands to do your work. I give you my feet to go your way. I give you my eyes to see as you do. I give you my tongue to speak your words. I give you my mind that you may think in me. I give you my spirit that you may pray in me. Above all, I give you my heart that you may love in me. . . . I give you my whole self that you may grow in me, so that it is you, Lord Jesus, who live and work and pray in me.[6]

A DEEPER REFLECTION
Aunt Zonia's Hands

Here's the church, here's the steeple, open the door . . . Oops. Let me reconfigure my fingers: here's the church, here's the steeple, open the door, and see all the people! "I believe in the holy catholic church." The church isn't a building. It's people. Before we had sanctuaries, budgets, committees, and bulletins, the Church was some people and the risen Christ. The people I first pastored after seminary recounted their most sacred moment: one Saturday night, a furnace spill turned the steeple and then the entire white A-frame wooden sanctuary into an inferno. Word spread, and by dawn they were all holding hands in a circle around the blackened timbers, not bothering to fight back the tears, saying good-bye to the holy temple where they had baptized their children and buried their parents, recognizing that "the Church is of God, and will be preserved to the end of time." That's not the church. We are the Church. See all the people, hands joined, fingers dancing in a tender salute to Jesus, to whom little ones belong.

Yet I think of my grandfather's devotion to the building. When he was a young man, a wind storm blew down his clapboard Baptist church in the middle of rural Stanly County, and he led a posse of believers who rounded up stiffer boards and hammered together a new temporary place (as all are temporary) for them to baptize their children and bury their parents. W. H. Vanstone was right: "Attachment to a Church building is by no means to be dismissed as sentimentality: it may well contain a profound, though possibly inarticulate, understanding of what that building is."[7] Go to Chartres, Cologne, Santiago de Compostela, or Durham; drive through rural America; study storefronts or factories transformed into churches in the inner cities of China or Lithuania: here is the Church, open the door, see the sacred space, the genius of humanity's greatest boast, the industry of labor, buildings that rise up and defy godlessness, silently voicing through the brick and mortar, "There is a God."

Little c—catholic

And there are invisible threads that weave us together, all of those churches, the storefronts, the cathedrals, the megachurches, fledgling house churches, speaking in countless tongues all over this planet, with wildly differing liturgies. I wonder whether more and more people have experienced the Church the way I have. Of all people, it would be the Southern Baptists I should thank for my being a Christian at all, although they nearly killed me. I was a bit of a heathen kid, so just after my family moved to Columbia, South Carolina, some Southern Baptist neighbors kept bugging me to go to church. Finally I agreed to go to a party for fifth-grade boys, not realizing it was at Lake Murray. Somehow I had missed learning how to swim, so I lied to my Baptist neighbors. "I have an ear infection. The doctor told me not to put my head under water." I learned a lesson that day: never underestimate how zealous Southern Baptists are to get you into the water! Four boys hoisted me up and tossed me into the drink, where I nearly drowned. A youth leader fished me out, and for obscure reasons I felt more inclined to thank Jesus for my rescue than to blame the Baptists for needing to be rescued.

My high school sweetheart was Lutheran, and her family insisted I worship with them. My college roommate was Episcopalian, and he dragged me to Young Life-type gatherings. A professor shoved me toward Duke and the Methodists; and although I am glad I am one still, it was at a Catholic retreat center that I had my closest encounter with Jesus. And my best clergy friends have been Presbyterian and Pentecostal. For me, the Church is "catholic"—little c, meaning united, not big C as in the Roman Catholic denomination. Speaking of which: the Catholics (big C) have been the subject of the most humiliating news stories in recent years. One of my dearest friends is a Catholic priest. He used to wear his collar out in public, thinking some opportunity might arise to love some random person in Christ's name: "Oh, Father, my mother is sick. Could you pray for her?" But not any more. Strangers in the grocery store make ugly remarks; recently one muttered, "Pervert!"

Friction in the Body

Tragically sad, but then the Church has always been something of an embarrassment to itself, and most assuredly an embarrassment to God. We major in the trivial and minor in the ridiculous. Our uncomfortable question when we utter the Creed should not be over the word "catholic." Rather, we should blush when we say "holy," for we are not very holy at all. We may wonder why anybody ever comes to a church, and why God didn't long ago file irrevocable divorce papers. But this is the miracle: "The Church is of God and will be preserved to the end of time"—not by its merits, not by its cleverness, but purely by the grace of God. Maybe this is, ironically enough, why people might be drawn to the Church. We come to God, not with merits or cleverness in hand, but as beggars, an embarrassment to ourselves; and when we poke our heads into the Church we see a silly bunch of calloused fingers wiggling about in the most sophomoric way—and there is room. See all the people. They point to a God whose crazed plan is to be present on earth through the unsightly, the ill-behaved. "Holy" then becomes a prayer, a desperate plea, a longing for what God might do with us.

God might wish we could understand our divisions in a warmer light. The real division in the Church is not between the Methodists and the Presbyterians or the Catholics and the Baptists. The most venal division appears right inside your own church. Ferocious disagreement within a denomination, even within a congregation, threatens to bleed the life out of us. Christians are in deep disagreement over homosexuality, politics, and most every other subject that matters. But can't there be a virtue to disagreement? When we notice that faithful, prayerful, intelligent believers disagree, instead of crossing our arms in rage and exiting the building, might we not embrace the sister, the brother, and at least try to understand how we can wind up at such contrary places? During the Civil War, Lincoln said, "Both sides read the same Bible, both pray—but the Almighty has his own purposes."[8] Disagreement can be the place where we can learn, the laboratory where we test out our half-baked ideas. We display the love and compassion for people who usually believe what they believe because they have been wounded some place. We exhibit a passion for truth that fears nothing; we rest securely only in Jesus, not in our pet thoughts about Jesus. I have not figured out all of God's truth at my age, and neither have you.

The psychiatrist Scott Peck names two valid reasons to get married: one is for the raising of children, and the other is "for the friction."[9] Friction, on the surface, seems like an evil to be avoided. But although friction is uncomfortable at first, if you stay with it, friction polishes. Sparks fly, heat rises, but the rough edges get smoothed out, fashioning something like a mirror. And we do not want merely to be a stone wall of conviction, but a mirror that might reflect God's image to others who see how we disagree, how we love, how we learn. Open the door, see all the people.

We Are Your Friends

We live in a milieu when people believe they can be Christian without the church; some would argue, "I can be a better Christian without the Church. I have enough problems, enough friction, without piling on the nonsense of Church folk." But aren't we in our culture a lonely people? Aren't we in fact the loneliest people who have ever walked across the stage of life on this planet? When people are really honest with me, they admit to an acute loneliness. You can be lonely at a party where everyone (you included) is laughing. You can be lonely in a meeting where your coworkers are plotting strategies. You can be lonely at home around the dinner table. The antidote to loneliness is not having more fun, or being in a bigger crowd. The only deep healing is a connection with God, and the connection with other people who want to go deep into their hearts, into subjects never touched at the water cooler or the football stadium. We are unfathomably desperate to know, and to be known, to love and to be loved, to let the fingers of my soul be intertwined with the fingers of yours, and we help one another toward God.

The Church's activities seem blandly trite, but our practices are the only viable way toward God, and out of our nagging loneliness. A fellow church member dies, and within hours we pull a hot casserole from the oven to deliver to people who aren't actually hungry due to their grief. But the casserole is a palpable message of love, curiously enough enabling the grieving family to exercise hospitality toward the other guests who come by the home unsure how to be of help, but determined to help just the same. Sometimes our efforts to love are pathetic—but even pathetic love is love. A couple of years ago I was sitting with a woman whose young husband had died. A casserole-bearer, anxious that the chicken divan was insufficient, added some words to the widow: "He's in a better place." She smiled politely, knowing he was lamely trying to be kind. After he left, she said to me, "I wish people wouldn't say he's in a better place. I suppose he is, but I really wanted him here with me." At our best, we Church members just show up. Don't explain God or try to soften the sharpness of the pain. It's the love, the being there, that matters. Consider the power of the little handwritten note: "I love you. I'm thinking of you. I'm praying for you." In *The Lord of the Rings,* the hobbit Merrie says, "You can trust us to stick with you through thick and thin, to the bitter end. And you can trust us to keep any secret of yours closer than you keep it yourself. But you cannot trust us to let you face trouble alone and go off without a word, because we are your friends, Frodo."[10] Thus the Church: you can't trust us to let you face your troubles alone. Open the door, see all the people.

You can't trust the church to let society face its troubles alone. To a society that is not of God, the Church has a vocation, although our mission is not always warmly welcomed. Archbishop Oscar Romero (whom thugs murdered for refusing to let El Salvador face its troubles alone) said:

This is the mission entrusted to the church, and it is a hard mission: to uproot sins from history, to uproot sins from the political order, to uproot sins from the economy, to uproot wherever they are. What a hard task! It has to meet with conflicts amid so much selfishness, so much pride, so much vanity, so many who have enthroned the reign of sin among us. The church must suffer for speaking the truth, for pointing out sin, for uprooting sin. No one wants to have a sore spot touched, and therefore a society with so many sores twitches when someone has the courage to touch it and say, "You have to treat that. You have to get rid of that." Believe in Christ and be converted.[11]

We live in a society that has so many sores. Our world is so wounded. Can we hide out behind these walls? Open the door, see all the people. We reach out. You have to treat that. Believe in Christ, be converted.

Broken

For we are broken ourselves—and so we know. We know weakness, we know brokenness, and therefore we know there is a God who is stronger than us. Little ones to him belong; they are weak, but he is strong. God can use us in spite of ourselves. Martin Luther said, "God can carve rotten wood, and God can ride the lame horse."[12] God does not require perfection, but just a willingness for us lame horses to be ridden, a readiness for us rotten timbers to be whittled down and built into the Church. Teresa of Avila reminds the lame and rotten, "Christ has no body now on earth but yours, no hands but yours, no feet but yours. Yours are the eyes through which the compassion of Christ looks out on a hurting world. Yours are the feet with which he goes about doing good. Yours are the hands with which he is to bless now."[13]

When I was a child, my parents dropped me off every summer in Oakboro, which is just on the outskirts of Frog Pond. I was farmed from house to house, and I loved staying with my great Aunt Zonia. I'm unsure how an orthopedist would diagnose my aunt: her hands were gnarled, underdeveloped somehow, fairly useless, awkward. You would think, "Oh, those are not good hands, they must be a problem." One night, a stiff fever and nausea laid me low. In my misery, Aunt Zonia stayed with me all night long, and with her twisted fingers she took a cold cloth and wiped my brow. She could have held back, thinking "Oh, my hands are bad hands, I wish I had soft, supple fingers instead of these cramped digits." But she took my small hands in her hands as best she could, and she didn't let go.

As a little boy, I discovered another hidden beauty in her hands. Returning home from the grocery store, she couldn't carry the bags into the house. She really needed me. No pretending: I was important at Aunt Zonia's house. I had a skill that made a difference. An odd quartet of hands the two of us shared: I could serve this woman who had served me. Years passed, and she phoned me from the hospital. I found her in intensive care, where she lay with a brain tumor, not expected to live long at all. Proud that I had grown up to be a man of the cloth, she asked "Will you preach my funeral? and will you pray for me?" I took her hands, or perhaps it was she who took mine, and we prayed. We offered her up to God. God can carve the rotten wood. God can ride the lame horse. We believe in the Church. We are the Body of Christ. We are the hands of Christ. We meet among these stones and we say here's the church, here's the steeple, open the door, and see all the people, wiggling in joy, holding hands, reaching out, signaling the presence of our Savior, Jesus Christ.

Notes

1. Quoted and discussed well in Colin W. Williams, *John Wesley's Theology Today* (Nashville: Abingdon Press, 1960), 16. In "The Catholic Spirit," *John Wesley*, ed. Albert C. Outler (New York: Oxford University Press, 1964), 101-3, Wesley declares, "A catholic spirit. . . . is not an indifference to *all* opinions. This is the spawn of hell. A man of a truly catholic spirit . . . is fixed as the sun in his judgment concerning the main branches of Christian doctrine. Go first and learn the first elements of the gospel of Christ, and then shall you learn to be of a truly catholic spirit. But while he is steadily fixed on his religious principles . . . his heart is enlarged toward all mankind; he embraces with strong and cordial affection neighbors and strangers, friends and enemies. For love alone gives the title to this character: catholic love is a catholic spirit."

2. Stanley Hauerwas, *In Good Company: The Church as Polis* (Notre Dame: University of Notre Dame Press, 1995), 9.

3. A lovely essay on Augustine, love and friendship may be found in *Becoming Friends: Worship, Justice, and the Practice of Christian Friendship* by Paul J. Wadell (Grand Rapids: Brazos, 2002), 77-95. Centuries later, Søren Kierkegaard wrote, "To

help another human being to love God is to love another man; to be helped by another human being to love God is to be loved" (*Works of Love*, trans. Howard and Edna Hong [New York: Harper, 1962], 113).

4. T. S. Eliot (in "Choruses from 'The Rock,'" *Collected Poems 1909–1962* [New York: Harcourt Brace Jovanovich, 1963], 160) asks, "Why should men love the Church? Why should they love her laws? She tells them of life and death, and of all that they would forget. She is tender where they would be hard, and hard where they like to be soft. She tells them of evil and sin, and other unpleasant facts."

5. "The Rules of the United Societies," *Wesley*, ed. Outler, 178.

6. Discussed in *Yours Are the Hands of Christ* by James Howell (Nashville: Upper Room Books, 1998), 120.

7. W. H. Vanstone, *Love's Endeavor, Love's Expense: The Response of Being to the Love of God* (London: Darton Longman Todd, 1977), 109.

8. From Lincoln's Second Inaugural Address.

9. M. Scott Peck, *A World Waiting to Be Born* (New York: Bantam, 1993), 105.

10. J. R. R. Tolkien, *The Fellowship of the Ring*, 115f.

11. Oscar Romero, *The Violence of Love*, trans. James R. Brockman (Farmington: Plough, 1998), 29-30.

12. A favorite saying of William Sloane Coffin, *Credo* (Louisville: Westminster John Knox Press, 2004), 20.

13. This traditional verse is the frontispiece of *Yours Are the Hands of Christ.*

Chapter Twelve

THE COMMUNION
OF THE SAINTS

LESSON 29

THE COMMUNION OF THE SAINTS
(PART 1)

Since we are surrounded by so great a cloud of witnesses,
let us lay aside every weight, and sin which clings so closely,
and let us run with perseverance the race that is set before us,
looking to Jesus. (Hebrews 12:1-2)

In many churches in Latin America, the roll is called in worship, including the names of members who have died, for whom someone in the room responds, "Presente!"

The first Christians worshiped in cemeteries, for they believed the deceased were very much alive, with God, and still in fellowship with the Church on earth. "'Til death do us part" simply does not apply to Church membership. God, mystically, across time and space, weaves all of his children together in a beautiful tapestry that glorifies God forever.

"The Communion of the Saints" also reminds us that we need heroes. Our culture throbs with celebrities—a constellation of stars glamorizing wealth, beauty, muscle, and sex. But aren't they seducing us away from God, and thinning us into superficial people? Celebrities feed our narcissism, our hedonism, our hollow existence. Heroes implicitly make demands, pushing us to live boldly for God. We need heroes for us to become good, or at least to become better. The very fact that a real, live human being managed to live in an exemplary way rids us of our excuse, "Oh, I'm only human." Some human lives have been faithful, courageous, Christlike. To say "Oh, she must be a saint" doesn't get us off the hook. What the saints have done, you and I can do.

By the grace of God, we have heroes who have embodied the faith; we remember their stories, we mimic their moves, we see God through them. "In his holy flirtation with the world, God occasionally drops a pocket handkerchief. These handkerchiefs are called saints" (Frederick Buechner).[1] The Church has its official saints (such as Francis of Assisi), and its unofficial, more familiar saints we should emulate (such as my grandfather). We look for lives in which "goodness makes a spectacle of itself" (John Navone).[2] If you want to be a friend of God, get to know the friends of God, those who have been "gripped" by Christ. For them, the Bible is not just a book casually discussed in the comfort of a classroom or easy chair. The Bible is to be lived out, "performed,"[3] like the script of a drama or symphony. The Bible is holy; but then those who practice what the Bible describes become holy.

Heroes do not live like everybody else. Saints are not 17 percent nicer than average, nor do they pray 23 percent more effectively. "It is the paradox of history that each generation is converted by the saint who contradicts it the most" (G. K. Chesterton).[4] We look for the Christian who lives against the grain, who sticks out, who makes us rethink, who may be laughed at by those immersed in our culture. And we recognize how we had better not "fit in," how following Jesus makes us downright odd. Saint Francis gave away all his wealth, yet his last words were, "I have done what is mine to do; now you must do what is yours to do." I'm not Francis; but then who is God calling me to be? Because we enjoy our place in the Communion of God's saints through space and time, we will settle for no less in our lives.

LESSON 30

THE COMMUNION OF THE SAINTS (PART 2)

For to me to live is Christ, and to die is gain. (Philippians 1:21)

Way back in lesson 1, we noticed that the word "creed" means "give my heart to," and that the words in the Creed never fully take on meaning until they are embodied in changed lives. Who better to portray the meaning of our beliefs than those who have acted out the faith in dramatic ways? The lives of the saints do not merely illustrate the Gospel; in a palpable way they *are* the Gospel, in the sense of the grace of God taking up residence in the reality of human life.

If we want to understand God as Maker of heaven and earth, we may look to St. Francis, who noticed God's handiwork in the skies, in sparrows and rodents, in royalty and lepers. Gerard Straub wrote:

> For Francis, beauty led to contemplation. In time, his love for the beauty of nature was transformed into a love of the beauty of God. God was Beauty and made everything beautiful. Francis began to see beauty even in ugliness. And Francis' response to Beauty was wonder and worship, and the growing knowledge that the earth was sanctified by the very fact of its creation.[5]

Beauty points us toward God, who is Beauty. Or in the words of Rowan Williams, "The beauty of worship, the beauty of holy lives, the beauty of lovely objects—none of these . . . is an end in itself. But that does not then mean they are a means to something else. They simply *are*, the overflowing of response, the super-abundance of love, and that is what is Godlike about them."[6]

Saint Francis is equally able to teach us about the Son of the Creator because he got up every morning and tried to imitate Jesus all day long.[7] He loved Jesus, not as a distant admirer, but so closely that he glued himself to the actions of the Jesus he loved. Thomas Dubay wrote that saints "live what they love; they are excited about the object of their love, and in their persons they unite truth, goodness and beauty."[8] Saints provide the clue that unlocks the meaning of the Creed, because the Creed is a cogent summary of the Bible, and the saints had this simplistic habit of taking the Bible literally. Not in the sense of arguing that the world was created in six days, but rather that the Bible was something you were supposed to *do*. For St. Francis, if the Bible said, "Sell all you have and give it to the poor," he naively went out and did so. The Scriptures are like a great script, and we are to be the actors; because of our unique personalities we will put our peculiar twist to our parts, but the Bible is the script and we stick to it, instead of inventing our own episodes that veer away from what the rest of the company is doing. Yes, we are clumsy actors, but aren't our foibles part of the beauty of God's work? that God's drama is all grace, shoving the inept like you and me onto the stage to bear the truth of the Gospel?

The most daunting lesson of the saints is the way they suffered. For centuries, Christians learned the Creed so they would be armed with an answer for interrogators in time of persecution. Countless martyrs preferred torture and death to even the slightest slippage in their devotion to the God extolled by the Creed. Their confidence, their hope, can calm us down, and grasp us with an urgency, a dogged determination to live as if "our citizenship is in heaven" (Philippians 3:20, AP).

A DEEPER REFLECTION
Fifteen Minutes

In a hotly contested race for the U.S. Senate in 1948, supporters of Lyndon Baines Johnson found support from some new voters— who were dead. Johnson and a handful of his campaign aides were out one night, fraudulently registering voters in a cemetery, when one worker came upon a certain tombstone, the letters worn over the decades, moss grown up over the marker. Skipping it to move on, he was upbraided by the leader of this expedition: "No, no, go back and register that person. He has as much right to vote as anybody else in this cemetery." We believe in the Communion of Saints. We Christians oddly believe that the dead have as much right to vote as the living, or perhaps a superior right to vote. Ridiculous as our belief may seem to the world, we believe they have come into their true citizenship, only after death.

In the Church, we certainly continue to care for those who have died. In *Animal Dreams*, Barbara Kingsolver tells about the town of Grace, where each year they celebrate the Day of the Dead. Everyone gathers in the village cemetery; they elaborately decorate the tombstones, strewing flowers all over the ground. They bring food; the children run; they sing and play games, a great festivity, all done with tender care. "It was a great comfort to see this attention lavished on the dead. In these families you would never stop being loved."[9] Christians have understood this since the beginning. The faithful in Rome gathered for worship in the catacombs outside the city. Burial places were not merely markers of sorrow and loss; tombs were portals into heaven, windows into the future. Worship at a gravesite seated believers near their brothers and sisters who had died and gone to be with God.

Reckless

They remembered the glory of Jesus' death, which Mary anticipated in the drama unveiled in John 12. It is mealtime, which always turned into one social *faux pas* after another for the prickly guest, Jesus. No one (to our knowledge) who ever had Jesus to dinner pronounced the evening smooth, stellar, or pleasant. But Jesus is more than a prophetic troubler this time. Shadows are gathering around Bethany, and Mary alone seems to intuit that Jesus is about to suffer and die. Occasionally excessive in her devotion to Jesus, she kneels at his feet, snaps off the top of a pottery flask, and begins to pour something on his feet. Onlookers are startled and then mortified when they see what it is—when they smell what it is. The aroma overwhelms the room, provoking someone to say (with mounting exasperation), "I recognize that! I think it's pure nard, imported from India. Why, my wife had some seven years ago. But look: it's soaking into the cracks in the floor, it's being wasted, it's too valuable, too precious. That oil must have cost maybe 300 denarii. I didn't earn that much all last year! And now it's been wasted; we can't get it back. We could have given it to the poor, but now it's just gone."

Mary exemplifies what it is to be a saint. Excessive, spontaneous, reckless. Saints do not come at Jesus in a measured, calculated way, as in "Oh, here: I have a little bit left over." After I finished writing a book on the lives of saints a few years ago, a friend read it and told me something I should have (and could have if it weren't too late!) featured in the book. The difference between saints and the rest of us is this: we get our lives organized over time; we have our commitments, our busy-ness, our work, playing tennis, socializing, tackling the mortgage, striving for a promotion, hauling the children to soccer. We aren't evil; we may even be doing some good. But we are pretty much booked—and then we come at God and say, "Hmm. I have five minutes and five dollars left over. I want to be a Christian, so here, God: I'll give you what I've got left." Then we feel fairly noble: "I gave what I had left to God." But saints, Christian heroes, say "God, it's all yours. It's all up for grabs. No prior commitment is sacred. Whatever you want me to do with all of my time, whatever you want me to do with all of my energy, whatever you want me to do with all of my possessions, my wealth, whatever it is that I have: God, it's all yours. I hold nothing back for myself."

Celebrities and Heroes

We do not see much of this in the land of the living; you almost always have to explore among the dead. What we have in the land of the living, instead of saints and heroes, are celebrities. Our eyes can barely take in the steady bombardment of Britney Spears, Shaquille O'Neal, Donald Trump, Jennifer Lopez, stars, more stars, glitz, more glitz. No one ever asks what our constant exposure to celebrities might be burrowing out of our souls. Christopher Lasch wrote that, in a narcissistic, self-pleasing culture, we welcome celebrities because we lack imagination and courage. How will Shaq and J-Lo help me to become good or wise? Celebrities flaunt a moral that cries, "Life is all about fun, consuming, purchasing, being cool, getting ahead, being rich and slick." Heroes (and saints) make demands on us. They exercise our imaginations, stretching us to become nobler, holier, more faithful. And if you have even a faint urge to be good, if you want to live your life for God, you have to turn off the tube, stop gawking at the celebrities, and find somebody else to mimic.

I coach my son's baseball team, and the fun of batting practice is watching each boy's choreography when he approaches the plate. The head turned, the bat cocked at a peculiar angle, every boy sporting a unique posture—but not really unique at all. A copycat stance: Nathan has his Jason Giambi imitation going, Noah has his Derek Jeter thing going, Melissa more of a throwback to Mickey Mantle. Every Christian needs a hero to mimic; if I could get his move down, if I could flash a bit of her style, then I might excel in the life of faith, holiness, and service. I stood in line with my oldest daughter so we could see Mother Teresa at the Charlotte Coliseum. She entered to cameras flashing, applause roaring, and on the huge TV screen that usually shows replays of Shaq's dunks, we saw her, two full feet shorter than Shaq, stooped with age, the feeding and tender care of literally thousands of Indian children etched upon the graceful folds of her wrinkled, smiling face. My daughter's eyes flew wide open, and she turned to me and said, "Daddy, she looks like somebody in the Bible."

Shrewd for her years, this eleven-year-old. Mother Teresa, like all saints, looked like somebody in the Bible, because she read the Bible, not as an interesting book for discussion. We do this: around a table, we open the Bible with friends and say, "Verse 7 sure is interesting, isn't it?" But the saints read verse 7 and bolted out into the street to do it. People like Mother Teresa, St. Francis and a holy host of others took the Bible literally—in the sense of taking it at face value as the script for life, as the map for where to go this morning, as the hourly prompter for this evening's schedule.

Jan Jordan

One of my favorite saints from recent times is Clarence Jordan, who earned a graduate degree in agriculture, but also owned and took with great seriousness a Bible, thinking (like Mother Teresa) that he was supposed to do what it said.[10] He read the book of Acts and noticed the first Christians were what we might think of as "communists," not atheistic operators of gulags, but people who had no private property. They shared everything in common, living together, pooling resources. Jordan decided he would take the Bible literally, so he bought a farm in rural Georgia and invited others with the same vision into the family of God—some white, some black. And he did this in the early 1950s, during the "Red scare" when McCarthy found communists under every rock, when Americans had not even begun their agonizing, bloody wrestling match toward civil rights and integration. You can imagine how pleased the Ku Klux

Klan was to have Jordan in the neighborhood. The harassment was relentless: almost ripened crops were torched, guns fired randomly into farm buildings, crosses burned beside the driveway.

But it was one thing for Jordan to choose to endure such persecution; it was another for an innocent child, and Jordan was raising a family. One day, Clarence's daughter, Jan, came home from school in tears. He asked, "Honey, what's wrong?" She said, "Oh, dad, a lot of the kids are mean, but there's this one boy named Bob Speck. Every time Bob sees me coming down the hallway, he comes up and knocks me down. He throws my books down the hallway. He says the ugliest words to me." Jordan said, "Jan, you've got long fingernails. Why don't you scratch his eyes out?" And she said, "Well, I thought about that, but I heard you say in your sermon that Jesus said we're supposed to love our enemy, so I thought I shouldn't scratch his eyes out." He said, "Well, I'll tell you what I'm going to do: tomorrow I'll go to the school, and I'm going to ask Jesus to excuse me from being a Christian for about fifteen minutes while I beat the daylights out of Bob Speck." But then Jan said, "Daddy, you can't do that." He said, "Why not?" She said, "You can't be excused from being a Christian for fifteen minutes."

Maybe the most crucial question for you and me is: how do I, in the pace of real life, excuse myself from being a Christian for fifteen minutes here and there? Maybe it's not to beat the daylights out of somebody. Maybe I'm just having a little fun. Maybe I forget to pray, or I'm too busy for the person in need. Maybe I'm just doing what everybody else does. But at the end of the day, don't we want to approach life with Jan Jordan's clarity? You can't be excused from being a Christian for fifteen minutes! You don't want little fifteen minute breaks from your faith; you don't want a single moment of separation from God. You want, somewhere inside, to be profligate, a tad reckless, like Mary, like Teresa, like Francis. You do not want your faith to be nothing but talk. Dorothy Day laid down the challenge when she said, "I have long since come to believe that people never mean half of what they say, and that it is best to disregard their talk and judge only their actions."[11]

Icons Around Us

To keep more fifteen-minute segments connected to God, to be more than a talker, to let our actions be judged, to dare great and little practical things for God, you need help. I discovered a curious kind of help in a practice developed by the early Christians who decorated their homes with icons, paintings of saints who meant a lot to them. In my home and office, I have a photograph of Mother Teresa, a painting of St. Francis, an icon of Dorothy Day, a poster of Martin Luther King, Jr., and a snapshot of my grandfather. I see these mystical friends, and looking at them reminds me to be good, humble, prayerful, zealous, holy.

And I like to think these images work in another way, which I can illustrate by a funny story. When Lisa and I were first married, we returned to her condominium for our first post-honeymoon night together. I slipped under the covers, lay my head on the pillow, and noticed on the nightstand (no more than eighteen inches from my nose) a stand-up 8½-by-11 photograph of two people smiling broadly: my in-laws. Forsaking my newlywed manners, I asked my bride, "Could we move this picture somewhere else?" In the same way, I sense in my icons and photos of heroes that the saints are not just there for me to observe, but also they are watching me. We believe in the Communion of Saints, who are not once-upon-a-time relics in the museum of religious folk, but a living presence, keeping an eye on me, caring about me, voting across space and time, changing my life. If Mother Teresa is somehow present and watching, then perhaps instead of indulging myself I will attend to someone who is lonely. If Papa Howell is somehow present and watching, then perhaps I pick up my Bible, get on my knees, and pray. If Dr. King and Dorothy Day are in the room, then perhaps I leave the room and knock on a door in the corridors of power and ask for some justice.

But I can't do it in five minutes with five bucks left over in my pocket. Mary came to Jesus with something she could not really afford, shocking everyone else, not bothering to count the cost. She just poured it all out for Jesus. You see, at the end of life you and I will land in some cemetery, casting the ultimate votes of our lives. Be very sure that God will not ask, "Hey, what did you do with the five minutes and the five bucks that you had left over?" Instead, God will ask, "What did you do with *all* of it? What did you do with all that I gave you, all those minutes, all those days, all the stuff, all the talents? Were you stingy? Did you hold back because . . . ? Or were you like Mary?" Remembering the right of the dead to vote, you may just pour it out, you surprise yourself with some extravagant gesture for God, you throw caution to the wind and do something down-right wasteful—but it's not really wasted because it's for God. We're part of this family of God where you never stop being loved, and we can trust in that. So we join hands with great heroes and saints through time, offering up our lives in praise and thanksgiving to our God. And then in the next fifteen minutes, we repeat ourselves. And also in the next fifteen minutes.

Notes

1. Frederick Buechner, *Wishful Thinking: A Seeker's ABC* (New York: Harper & Row, 1973), 83.

2. John Navone, *Enjoying God's Beauty* (Collegeville: Liturgical, 1999), xiii.

3. Nicholas Lash, "Performing the Scriptures," *Theology on the Way to Emmaus* (London: SCM, 1986), 37-46.

4. G. K. Chesterton, *Saint Thomas Aquinas* (Garden City, N.Y.: Image, 1956), 24.

5. Gerard Thomas Straub, *The Sun and Moon Over Assisi: A Personal Encounter with Francis and Clare* (Cincinnati: St. Anthony Messenger, 2000), 62.

6. Rowan Williams, *A Ray of Darkness: Sermons and Reflections* (Cambridge: Cowley, 1994), 25.

7. G. K. Chesterton, *Saint Francis of Assisi* (Garden City: Image, 1957), 117-18: "It is really very enlightening to realise that Christ was like St. Francis. . . . St. Francis is the mirror of Christ rather as the moon is the mirror of the sun. The moon is much smaller than the sun, but it is also much nearer to us; and being less vivid it is more visible. Exactly in the same sense St. Francis is nearer to us, and being a mere man like ourselves is in that sense more imaginable."

8. Thomas Dubay, *The Evidential Power of Beauty* (San Francisco: Ignatius, 1999), 331.

9. Barbara Kingsolver, *Animal Dreams* (New York: HarperCollins, 1990), 163.

10. See my summary of Jordan's life, with references to further reading, in *Servants, Misfits and Martyrs: Saints and Their Stories* (Nashville: Upper Room, 1999), 25-30, 47-52.

11. Robert Coles, *Dorothy Day: A Radical Devotion* (Reading: Addison-Wesley, 1987), 36.

Chapter   Thirteen

THE FORGIVENESS OF SINS

LESSON 31
FORGIVENESS (PART 1)

*Forgive us our trespasses, as we forgive those who trespass
against us. (Matthew 6:12)*

Nothing is more poorly understood, or more desperately
needed, than forgiveness. The whole point of Christianity
is reconciliation—forgiveness between God and us, and
between one another. We are the only organization crazy
enough to be constituted by the practice of the confession of
sin.[1] Yet in modern times, some dark clouds of confusion have
drifted in to block the hopeful sunlight of forgiveness. On our side,
we frankly don't think we need much forgiveness. We are so prac-
ticed at self-justification, at rationalizing and explaining. We feel
entitled. I'm owed a good life, and if I don't get it, I get busy blam-
ing somebody.

But isn't all that a façade? Deep inside, don't you crave mercy, to
be loved despite your craziness, to be handled tenderly? And don't
we need to be tender, merciful, forgiving to others? "When death,
the great Reconciler, has come, it is never our tenderness that we
repent of, but our severity" (George Eliot).[2] We are such hard, tough,
cool, smooth, crusty people—but how sad, how tragic. Hope begins
when we lean into forgiveness, when we fess up and admit "I have

sinned" against God, against others, and usually most painfully against those we love the most. We need mercy.

A terrible confusion that muddies things: forgiveness, we foolishly think, means saying "Oh, it doesn't matter." But forgiveness is when we say "This matters so much we've got to do something about it. We've got to reconcile." Reconciliation isn't easy. Forgiveness is the hardest work. You have to dig stuff up and wrestle with it. You must be brutally honest, yet kind. You listen deeply enough to understand those hidden causes of what has gone on between you and the other person.

Forgiveness isn't always a warm fuzzy feeling. If you forgive me, it doesn't mean you feel like showering me with hugs and kisses. Forgiveness is a decision, a commitment to look at me through God's eyes, to stick with me. In broken families, this is a daunting challenge: you may forgive a parent, or a spouse, but this does not require one ounce of gushy emotion. Greg Jones underlines the practicality of forgiveness:

> Forgiveness is not so much a word spoken, or a feeling felt, as it is an embodied way of life in an ever-deepening friendship with God and others. . . . Forgiveness ought not simply be focused on the absolution of guilt; rather, it ought to be focused on the reconciliation of brokenness, the restoration of communion.[3]

Forgiveness is not getting out of court with no more than a slap on the wrist. Forgiveness moves toward a new, restored relationship.

Forgiveness is an alien concept for us who've been taught to be strong, to stand up for ourselves, to live a steely "It's all up to me" life; for forgiveness happens when I assume a posture of weakness, when I give up my "rights," when I give up being right. Reconciliation: you cannot accomplish this for yourself, or by yourself. You need the Spirit of God; you need somebody outside yourself.

For there is always a vertical and a horizontal dimension to forgiveness. It is one thing to grapple with forgiveness before God, which feels different from forgiveness with another person— although the two are intimately, inextricably woven together.[4] My failure to probe toward forgiveness with another person can erect a massive barrier between me and God; and the breakdown in my sense of forgiveness with God is precisely what inhibits me moving toward reconciliation with someone else. We will take these two dimensions up over the next pair of lessons.

LESSON 32
FORGIVENESS (PART 2)

Christ reconciled us to himself and gave us the ministry of reconciliation. (2 Corinthians 5:18)

"I bruise you, you bruise me, we both bruise too easily" sang Art Garfunkel. Something goes wrong between people, and in our culture of complaint, blame, and entitlement, forgiveness is increasingly elusive, yet is a craft needed more desperately now than ever. Forgiveness is a skill, something you practice, a practical strategy of action, not merely an emotion.

We may avoid the work of forgiveness, not merely because it's hard work, but because there can be something darkly delicious about an unhealed grievance, as Buechner probingly explains:

> To lick your wounds, to smack your lips over grievances long past, to roll over your tongue the prospect of bitter confrontations still to come, to savor to the last toothsome morsel both the pain you are given and the pain you are giving back—in many ways, it is a feast fit for a king. The chief drawback is that what you are wolfing down is yourself. The skeleton at the end of the feast is you.[5]

God wired us so that dealing with a fractured relationship is not only healthy for me and the other person. More stunning, when we tell the truth, when we get beyond blame, when we let love's creative power reclaim a lost relationship, we actually mirror what God does for us. Martin Luther King, Jr. gave us shrewd advice, but also described how God befriends us: "Love is the only force capable of transforming an enemy into a friend. We never get rid of an enemy by meeting hate with hate; we get rid of an enemy by getting rid of enmity. By its very nature, hate destroys and tears down; by its very nature, love creates and builds up."[6]

The building-up process is interesting: in Old Testament law, if I have sinned against you, the first thing I must do is make reparation; if I steal your sheep, I must replace it. But I also make a sacrifice to God of something precious to myself—such as my best ram—so next time I'll think twice before eyeing your sheep. The priest would cut that sacrificial ram open and let the blood run down over the stone altar. They believed the power of God was sealed up inside blood; so by shedding blood, God's healing power was released— and they knew they needed it. Usually, when we have hurt someone deeply, no reparation can quite overcome the rift between us. Some residual distance lingers, no matter how hard we try to forgive. To close that gap, to bring healing beyond what we are capable of, God's power must enter in. Israel slaughtered animals to tap the divine power. We look to Jesus and seek out the power of his Spirit unleashed when Jesus was crucified and was raised.

This is a miracle: God's power can produce forgiveness when we cannot muster any on our own. God's power can even devise reconciliation between you and someone who has been dead for some time; often our most poignant regrets involve someone with whom it seems to be too late. But God can bring healing and peace. Even when the wrong done is unspeakably horrible: we can forgive, or rather, we can "believe in forgiveness," which really is God's. A biblical Greek word translated "forgive," *aphiemi* (pronounced ah-fee-ay-me), means quite simply to open your hand and let go of something you have been gripping tightly. We hold old hurts close to our hearts; they are corrosive, and they poison. But by the grace of God we can let them go, just as God has let ours go. We believe in forgiveness.

LESSON 33
FORGIVENESS (PART 3)

Jesus said, "Father, forgive them; for they know not what they do."
(Luke 23:34)

As we try to make sense of Jesus' Holy Week mission, we need a deeper understanding on an ultimate question: What is our problem?

What is the human predicament? Society says: your problem is, you aren't having enough fun, you lack fulfillment, you could use more money, and maybe God will help you. But guilt? The need for forgiveness? To modern folk, talk of sin, guilt, and forgiveness smacks of negative, unhealthy thinking. Instead of seeking forgiveness, some people have a hard time forgiving God for letting them down.

Totally at odds with our positive-thinking, pleasure-seeking culture, the Bible tells the truth, diagnosing us as having twin troubles, a dual predicament. We are mortal, and we are sinful. Jesus stormed Jerusalem to resolve both issues. First, sin. I may see myself as "a pretty good person"; we may suspect that God grades on the curve. But every day, in so many ways, with creativity and stubbornness, we sin, we turn away from God. I live for me, instead of for God. I do my will, deaf to God's will, or I brand my will as if it were God's will. I bow down and worship things and people that are not God; my mind is a nonstop "factory of idols" (as Calvin put it). We owe God constant holiness and focused loyalty, and we are deeply in arrears.

We owe God? Yes, but not the way I owe the IRS! We owe God the way a flower is in debt to the sunshine and rain, the way a cello is in debt to Mozart, the way I am in debt to my child who runs up and hugs me. We are not under investigation by a God who is touchy or nitpicky. God is brokenhearted over our waywardness, the way the tenderest parent weeps over a child's self-destruction. Wolfhart Pannenberg wrote: "Sin means going astray, failing to find the source of life in our search for life. . . . The point is not primarily individual faults; it is rather the faulty foundation of our existence as a whole, which merely finds expression in this or that mistaken attitude or concrete fault."[7] I do something I shouldn't, but then I do it again, and it becomes a habit; before long my will is chained, and I am no longer free to stop doing it. We are free, but we have squandered our freedom, letting it get shackled to a train-wreck about to happen.

But how nonsensical! How stupid! We rush away from God, who is literally dying to give us life and deep joy. Lash is right: "Sin makes no sense, and therefore its forgiveness is difficult to understand."[8] Forgiveness is so alien to us. Our culture says "Assign blame, get even, be fair, dole out just deserts." But God says there is another way to relate, and it begins between God and me and you: forgiveness, inherently unfair, undeserved, undercutting blame. If you say, "Forgiveness is unrealistic," you had better pray you are wrong. We may thank God that Jesus let himself be crushed in the gears of blame, for otherwise you and I have no hope at all. As long as we get stuck on blame, rights, and fairness, we will miss out on the most beautiful treasure, forgiveness.

When he spoke mercifully about the South, Lincoln said to a shocked listener, "Madam, do I not destroy my enemies when I make them my friends?" God's forgiveness is not indulgent; God destroys—not me, but the enemy in me: "God must be inexorable toward our sin, not because He is just, but because He is loving; not in spite of His love, but because of His love" (D. M. Baillie).[9] God invades and destroys the dark gap dividing us from God; and so, God destroys death itself.

A DEEPER REFLECTION
Only in This Way Can We Be Whole Again

The Epistle to the Hebrews: a book of soaring wonder and mystifying complexity! Let us hear one of its treasured moments.

> For we have not a high priest who is unable to sympathize with our weaknesses, but one who in every respect has been tempted as we are, yet without sinning. Let us then with confidence draw near to the throne of grace, that we may receive mercy and find grace to help in time of need. (Hebrews 4:15-16)

An old-fashioned "three-point sermon" may be in order. First, let us think about temptation; second, forgiveness; and then third, forgiveness again.

Temptation

The challenge of life with God, the relentless pressure on those who would love and serve God, is that temptation lurks around every corner, behind rocks, and even steps out into the bright light

142

of day, which would be no problem were we not so temptable! Tragically, we secretly relish the moment of temptation. The anticipation is titillating, and as society says life is about the indulgence of desire, our yearning cozies up to what the Church has historically taught were the "seven deadly sins": greed, lust, pride, gluttony, sloth, anger, and envy. We live in a society that permits everything and forgives nothing; but we will never be whole until we realize there are things God does not permit, and therefore that God can forgive everything.

We must understand the devil's strategy. The arsenal of temptation is subtle, deceptive. Lurking inside evil is a little perverted taste of the good; a lie only works because it lures you with a slice of truth. If evil mimics good, if the lie is a parody of truth, then we must be vigilant, and absolutely ruthless in boring down into the core of whatever we face. We beg God for a keener diagnostic eye. We assess our desires so that, instead of rushing to satisfy each and every one, we unmask quite a few as temptations to be fled. Not that desire is itself wicked. Church is not the anti-desire squadron, pouring cold water on desire. C. S. Lewis wisely suggested that the problem is not that our desires are too strong. Rather, our desires are too weak. We settle for far less than what God wants for us.[10] To strengthen desire, we must beware temptation, which appeals to our dark side, reminding us that we have a dark side, that we are wired with an embarrassing proclivity to be suckered into plunging headlong away from God and into self-destruction. Our most humble, urgent prayer must be, "Lead us not into temptation."

Can Jesus sympathize? Has he been "in every respect tempted as we are"? Robertson Davies mused that Jesus never had to cope with old age. Jesus never had to deal with marriage or parenting. When I was single, I would watch haggard parents dragging into church with their little urchins howling, and with a shrug I would resist asking, "Can't you control your children?" Now, having dragged my own three urchins various places, I realize the answer is "no." I was unable to sympathize. Can Jesus? Surely Jesus was wiser, was more able to get inside other people's skin; the glory of the incarnation is precisely that Jesus got inside our skin! He knows the answer to "Can't you control your children?" is "no." God does not control or manipulate us, so we are free to succumb to temptation, which is why we need this high priest.

Jesus can sympathize. Instead of swatting foes away by lifting his brow, he became vulnerable. Inside our skin, Jesus was deserted by the very people who said they loved him. He suffered pain, death, loss; he wept, he was ferociously tempted by the devil himself. As Jesus wielded light-years more power than you and I can wield, the lure to use it for himself must have been gargantuan. By an astonishing will, by always saying to God, "Not my will, but your will be done," Jesus held temptation at bay—and he did not yield because of his personal mission: he loved me, he loved you so much. He came down so we could go up, so he could help in time of need.

Consider that awful moment in the *Iliad,* when Hector and Achilles were engaged in combat. Pallas deceived Hector, offering him a spear; but when Hector turned for the spear, he grabbed nothing but air. There was no spear, there was no help, and Achilles killed the unarmed Hector. In our time of need, in the hour of temptation, we cannot win the battle alone; but we are never deceived, and never alone. We turn to Christ, and he is there. We have a great high priest. There is power. There is mercy.

Forgiveness

In modern times, we have drifted into a lackadaisical mind-set, fantasizing that our debt is tiny, or nonexistent. We have assumed God is indulgent, or as Voltaire glibly said, "God will forgive me; that's his job." Or problems seemingly bigger than sin loom before us. Reynolds Price tells of being diagnosed with a malignant tumor in his spine. Sleeping one night, he had a vivid dream of Jesus by the Sea of Galilee, who spoke to Price, declaring, "Your sins are forgiven." Quite understandably, he replied, "It's not my sins I'm worried about."[11]

Yet maybe we should be far more worried about sin than we are. We get curved in on ourselves. We are cold when it comes to the things of God. We go traipsing off from God, doing our own thing, rarely asking where God might actually be calling us to go. We are unholy. If we ever see the poor, we yawn, or blame them for the straits they've gotten themselves into. The very notion of sin feels outmoded to us, and we have multiple ways to rename or explain away sin that the Bible and the Church have tried valiantly to cure for centuries. Adultery is now "an affair," a fully understandable stab at fulfillment. Consumer capitalism is all about coveting, lust, greed, pride, gluttony, and sloth; and if the Church warns us of the grave perils hidden therein, people just laugh, or a few yawns are elicited. Albert Camus described most of us when he said, "I had pretty much lost the habit of analyzing myself."[12]

Should we analyze ourselves (and we may be sure, God has not lost the habit of analyzing us), we would have to agree with T. S. Eliot's unflattering portrait of our moral selves in the poem "East Coker": inside, we have "shabby equipment, forever deteriorating"; inside, we harbor "undisciplined squads of emotion" (or as C. S. Lewis put it, "a zoo of lusts"). In the light of the Cross of Christ, we are stricken with grief over our waywardness. What wondrous love is this? We would be silly to stand with Garrison Keillor's residents of Lake Wobegon, where everyone is merely "above average." "Love so amazing, so divine, demands my soul, my life, my all."

Our relationship with God is fractured and hangs in need of attention, some radical surgery. The gulf is immense. In 1990, an ossuary (a limestone box in which the bones of deceased were buried) was discovered bearing the name Caiaphas, and we can be fairly certain that these are the remains of the high priest during the final days of Jesus' life. The high priest was the chief of religious life, and the primal function of the temple was the provision of forgiveness. The Latin word for priest, *pontifex,* literally means "bridge-builder." Across the shadowy gulf sin burrows out between us and God, a bridge must be built, and as Catherine of Siena put it, the only timbers that can form such a bridge are the beams of the cross of Christ.[13] Ironically, Jesus proved to be the pontifex, not Caiaphas.

In *Beach Music,* Pat Conroy writes of Lucy, whose own brother is the priest administering her last rites:

> For a solid week he had prayed and fasted for his sister. His faith was unshakable, and he believed that any of Lucy's sins were light-weight to the God who had wept his way through this unendurable century. The entire monastery had stockpiled prayers for Lucy. She would enter paradise buoyed up on a field of praise, well recommended.[14]

Indeed. Our sins are lightweight to the God who weeps over us, as heavy as the agony of Jesus on the Cross, as light as a whispered prayer. We go before God, not with strong legs and an above-average record; rather, we discover we are well-recommended, startlingly undeserved. Jesus took all our sin, our sophomoric foolishness, our self-indulgence, our recklessness, our loneliness, our woundedness, our very death, and bears us up on the beams of his amazing grace. He is able to sympathize with our weakness. There is mercy in our hour of need.

Forgiveness

Then there is also forgiveness. We may wish Jesus had never tucked that very familiar petition into the Lord's Prayer: "Forgive us our trespasses, as we forgive those who trespass against us." We Methodists who trespass (and we Presbyterians who pile up debts) are left with no wiggle room when we seek forgiveness, for Jesus wrapped our hope of forgiveness from God in with the way we forgive other people. We may prefer to plead extenuating circumstances: "God, if you only understood how miserably he treated me, if you only grasped the immensity of her crime." But God understands, and so did St. Augustine, who reminded us that the sword of anger you thrust toward your neighbor first passes through your own heart. This is why Pope John Paul II forgave his would-be assassin. This is why black South Africans looked into the faces of white policemen who had tortured and killed family members and announced "I forgive you" at the "Truth and Reconciliation" trials. This is why our world is doomed to random violence until we learn reconciliation instead of retaliation.

Unforgiven sin between us tangles us up in some barbed wire that lacerates the soul. This is hard, and countercultural, for we live in a society of blame. Politicians know whom to blame; couples wrangle and blame the flawed spouse; institutions get blamed for all evils; citizens leap into court to blame someone for something. But the Gospel would liberate us from the steel trap of blame. In John Irving's *The World According to Garp*, Helen and John have wounded each other in unspeakable ways (actually, they are literally unable to speak because of injuries incurred in an accident). John, after days of raging silence, takes a slip of paper, scribbles on it, and hands it to his estranged wife: "I don't blame you." After a while, he hands her another slip: "I don't blame me either." And then a third: "Only in this way can we be whole again."[15]

Forgiveness is letting blame go, being drawn toward being whole again. Marriages founder on these rocks, as we let little sins fester, or we superficially "kiss and make up." In forgiveness, we deal with the hurt, the dysfunction, but we deal with it in a house of mercy. The absurdity of forgiveness is the relinquishment of our rights, the refusal to balance accounts. Forgiveness gets inside the other person's skin. We read 1 Corinthians 13 at weddings, and people grin sweetly over the seemingly syrupy words about love. But Paul dared to suggest that "love bears all things, hopes all things." Not "love bears most things, love hopes for a certain period of time." We are invited to be high priests, to be bridge builders, to be Christ to one another, to sympathize. In the comedy film *Bruce Almighty,* the insensitive, knuckleheaded Bruce is finally broken down by life, brokenhearted over squandering his relationship with Grace—and in his humbled misery finds himself face to face with God, who asks, "What do you really want, Bruce? Do you want Grace back?" Bruce, finally understanding, surprises even God by saying "No. I want her to meet somebody who will love her, who will give her what she deserved from me. I want her to meet someone who will see her the way I see her now—through your eyes."

Just as marriages need forgiveness, parents and children require considerable forgiveness. Conroy spoke of larceny as not being such an awful crime—"unless your childhood was the item stolen."[16] So many people live with a gaping hole where a dad or mom should have been. Sometimes this unreconciled darkness is carried down into the grave—and the miracle of the Gospel is that we can visit the cemetery, lay down a flower, and say what we may not have said: "I forgive you." Not "I have warm fuzzy feelings, or what you did was okay, but I let it go, I relinquish my anger, my hurt."

God's family on this planet needs forgiveness. We cannot veer into the political arena too daringly in this sermon, but Dietrich Bonhoeffer was right when he said, "There can only be peace when it does not rest on lies and injustice. . . . The forgiveness of sins still remains the sole ground of all peace."[17] Ron Silver, at the Republican National Convention in 2004, spoke out on Iraq and others in the Arab world and announced, "We will never forgive. We will never forget." But this thought, "We will never forgive," never crosses God Almighty's mind. Because of Jesus, we who would be Christian have no option but to pray earnestly for the forgiveness of even our vilest enemies. Lies cannot bring peace. Truth is the beginning of peace, in our hearts, and in the world. And peace is forever impossible unless we engage in forgiveness—in our hearts, in our relationships, in our families, and in the world.

Sometimes we just need to forgive life. Stuff happens, the cards are dealt, our dreams are dust, we lose what we could not bear to lose, the disappointment is stacked high, the years stretch out behind us, the sadness is heavy. Without God, life is unforgivable. But when we look back and see the cross staked in the middle of it all, we can even forgive life, for we have a high priest who died young and unjustly, who was despised and rejected, who is able to sympathize; so we "with confidence draw near to the throne of grace, that we may receive mercy and find grace to help in time of need" (Hebrews 4:16). I suspect that for you, and for me, that time of need is now. Draw near. Be drawn near to the throne of grace. Open your hand, let that sin, that wound, that grievance you clutch so tightly—just open your hand and let it fall into the outstretched, crucified hands of Jesus. Watch his hands. Hear him say to you, "Let us pray." We fold our hands together, and pray, "Lead us not into temptation. Forgive us our trespasses, as we forgive those who trespass against us." Then we know: there is mercy, grace, help, hope.

Notes

1. Stanley Hauerwas, *In Good Company: The Church as Polis* (Notre Dame: University of Notre Dame Press, 1995), 5.

2. George Eliot, *Adam Bede* (New York: Signet, 1961), 62.

3. L. Gregory Jones, *Embodying Forgiveness: A Theological Analysis* (Grand Rapids: Eerdmans, 1995), xii.

4. Cynthia Rigby, "Reviving Forgiveness," in *Exploring & Proclaiming the Apostles' Creed*, ed. Roger E. Van Harn (Grand Rapids: Eerdmans, 2004), 255, notices how the Creed prevents us from thinking forgiveness is merely something I derive from God: "The 'forgiveness of sins' seems to be in the wrong place. Shouldn't it be in one of the first two articles? Doesn't it better describe the work of the 'almighty Father' or 'Jesus Christ'? (After all, it's clear that *they are* the ones who handle forgiveness.) Instead, 'forgiveness of sins' comes near the end, in the section about the Holy Spirit's work in the context of the Christian community. Forgiveness seems to be a trademark of the communion of saints, an aspect of what it is to be holy. Leaving forgiveness to God, then, does not appear to be an option."

5. Frederick Buechner, *Wishful Thinking: A Seeker's ABC* (New York: Harper & Row, 1973), 29.

6. Martin Luther King, Jr., "Strength to Love," in *A Testament of Hope: The Essential Writings of Martin Luther King, Jr.,* ed. James Melvin Washington (San Francisco: Harper & Row, 1986), 61.

7. Wolfhart Pannenberg, *The Apostles' Creed in the Light of Today's Questions,* trans. Margaret Kohl (Eugene: Wipf and Stock, 1972), 164.

8. Nicholas Lash, *Believing Three Ways in One God: A Reading of the Apostles' Creed* (Notre Dame: University of Notre Dame Press, 1992), 116.

9. D. M. Baillie, *God Was in Christ: An Essay on Incarnation and Atonement* (New York: Charles Scribner's Sons, 1948), 173.

10. C. S. Lewis, *The Weight of Glory* (New York: Simon & Schuster, 1996), 26. His words, from a sermon preached at Oxford in 1941, "The Weight of Glory," were, "If we consider the unblushing promises of reward and the staggering nature of the rewards promised in the Gospels, it would seem that Our Lord finds our desires not too strong, but too weak. We are half-hearted creatures, fooling about with drink and sex and ambition, when infinite joy is offered us, like an ignorant child who wants to go on making mud pies in a slum because he cannot imagine what is meant by the offer of a holiday at the sea. We are far too easily pleased."

11. Reynolds Price, *A Whole New Life* (New York: Scribner's, 1982), 43; the longer story of the dream is lovely, and includes Jesus scooping handfuls of water from the sea to bathe Price.

12. Albert Camus, *The Fall* (New York: Vintage, 1991).

13. Catherine of Siena, *The Dialogue,* ed. Richard Payne (New York: Paulist, 1980).

14. Pat Conroy, *Beach Music* (New York: Doubleday, 1995), 609.

15. John Irving, *The World According to Garp* (New York: Ballantine, 1976), 380-81.

16. Pat Conroy, *The Prince of Tides* (New York: Bantam, 1987), 282.

17. Dietrich Bonhoeffer, *No Rusty Swords,* trans. John Bowden (New York: Harper & Row, 1956), 168, discussed probingly by Stanley Hauerwas, *Performing the Faith: Bonhoeffer and the Practice of Nonviolence* (Grand Rapids: Brazos, 2004).

Chapter Fourteen

THE RESURRECTION OF THE BODY AND THE LIFE EVERLASTING

LESSON 34

THE RESURRECTION OF THE BODY (PART 1)

While we were weak, at the right time, Christ died for the ungodly. . . . Now that we have been justified by his blood, we will be saved through him. (Romans 5:6, 9, AP)

Easter begins in a cemetery. Before resurrection happens, there is death; you cannot get to Easter without lingering over Good Friday. The startling, scandalous message of the Bible is that God miraculously, impossibly entered into the flesh we know too well; Jesus suffered a horrific death, as we have already recognized in lessons 15 through 17. And we are not immaterial souls living temporarily encased in a body; I am my body, and just as Jesus' body was raised (albeit in a transformed state), so my body will be raised. We do not believe in the immortality of the soul, but in the resurrection of the body, as we have discussed in lesson 21. To these reflections we add a few thoughts now.

Christianity is unique among the religions of the world in suggesting, not merely the intellectually nonsensical idea that God became flesh, but also that instead of donning some perfected, impenetrable flesh, instead of trouncing all his foes with a militaristic athleticism, Jesus submitted to evil people and let himself suffer grotesquely, dying the most humiliating, embarrassing death imaginable. God's love for us was (and is) so immense that God could not bear for us to endure our pain, agony, desolation, and even death alone. God is in the thick of whatever trouble we see, bearing it from the inside out. For me, this is the great proof of the worth of Christianity, even its surpassing value as one faith among many.

Why did Jesus suffer? We speak of the "passion" of Christ. "Passion" comes from the Latin word *patior,* meaning "to suffer, endure, bear." Christ endured, bore suffering. Yet "passion" has another connotation: strong emotion, investment in a cause, commitment. Jesus did what he did "with a passion." With a zealous devotion to God, with an unquenchable love for you and me, Jesus passionately embraced his passion. We may recall again St. Francis's prayer: "My Lord Jesus Christ, two graces I ask of you before I die: that I may feel, in my soul and body, as far as possible, that sorrow which you, tender Jesus, underwent in the hour of your most bitter passion; and that I may feel in my heart, as far as possible, the abundance of love with which you, son of God, were inflamed, so as willingly to undergo such a great passion for us sinners." Only this kind of love explains the resurrection.

Jesus suffered as the ultimate sacrifice for our sin, as the palpable demonstration of God's love, as he engaged in combat against evil and death. "For God so loved the world that he gave his only Son" (John 3:16). In this moment we see God; in this darkest of hours God is brightly glorified. On the cross, God seems absent. But there God is most surely present. God's love made vulnerable, risking everything, suffering as love inevitably suffers—and yet since it is this one who suffers, history is turned upside down. In those hours of agony on Good Friday, Jesus was taking onto his own heart all of the misery, the sin, the sorrow, the loneliness, the hopelessness of all people in all ages. All are held tightly by his outstretched arms close to the bosom of God. The window to God's heart flung open, the curtain ripped asunder, our forgiveness not merely offered but embodied, our hope assured.

152

LESSON 35

THE RESURRECTION OF THE BODY (PART 2)

If Christ has not been raised, your faith is futile; . . . If for this life only we have hoped in Christ, we are of all [people] most to be pitied. (1 Corinthians 15:17, 19)

Easter is so familiar in our culture, even as a popular holiday for people with not the slightest inclination toward Christianity, that it is easy for us to underestimate the shock, the miracle, how stupendously existence is turned upside down because Jesus did not stay in his tomb the way people are supposed to. And the notion of living on beyond death is blandly assumed, even by otherwise irreligious folk; if we glibly assume all dogs go to heaven, then we miss the startling wonder of the Creed's final word.

The question to be addressed is not merely whether the story of Jesus' resurrection is true. The philosopher Søren Kierkegaard polled people on the streets of Copenhagen, asking "Do you believe Jesus was raised?" Virtually all said yes, but no one could point to the slightest difference this "fact" made, going about their business as if no resurrection had happened.

For resurrection to open some doors, you need some imagination; you open yourself to a truth bigger than yourself, fathoming that your greatest need is something you could not begin to achieve for yourself. Resurrection really is about love, being loved by a God for whom the grave is no barrier. Resurrection is not the grand prize for a life well-lived, and resurrection is not what Mitch Albom squashes it down to in *The Five People You Meet in Heaven:* Heaven is not when you learn your life really was better than you thought, discovering that "Hey, I was a pretty good person," that it really is "a wonderful life" (George Bailey–style).[1] No five people can provide meaning. Only one, only God, matters ultimately in the end. Heaven is not "You did it!" but "Treasure this fantastic, undeserved gift."

God's love for you is so immense, that the relationship you begin now is something God cannot bear to see concluded at the moment you breathe your last; so God continues to love you and to draw you into a far more focused relationship where confusion is no more. Eternal life is not a really long continuation of this life, where you play constant golf with birdies every hole, or where you add no pounds from devouring delectable chocolate éclairs. Heaven is intimacy with God, the old life and its corruptions long forgotten, a new life of understanding; and frankly, you spend your time praising God. People long to see loved ones in heaven whom they have missed—and we shall! But remember how Dante concluded *The Divine Comedy:* finally reaching heaven, he sees his beloved Beatrice. She turns, smiles in welcome, and then the two of them, side by side, turn to praise God forever.

Karl Barth wrote that, because of the resurrection, you just can't walk around with a sour look on your face. You also can't live for yourself. You can't slavishly indulge in our culture, consuming, doing as you wish. The world, your life, and the life of everyone around you, is in God's hands—so we follow God now, totally, joyfully. Whatever eternal life is like, we may as well practice for it right now. In heaven, money means zilch, there are no racial divisions, love is tender and vocal, holiness and service are habitual, we are at peace. We practice, and we trust, not knowing precisely what our future holds. We trust a God who has devised a future for us that will exceed our grandest fantasies; and whatever that future holds, it will be enough, because we know who will be there before we get there: our risen Lord and Savior Jesus Christ.

A DEEPER REFLECTION
If God Should Surprise

A decade ago, I preached in a college community, our services frequented by bright, inquisitive college students. The smartest among them (or so the dean reported to me) was a cynic, his questions barbed, too smart for the Gospel, too smart for this preacher to handle any way but gingerly. One Sunday we extended an old-fashioned altar call, and a handful of worshipers stepped up to the altar for prayer. Among them was this smartest of students. He knelt, so absorbed in prayer that he did not budge even after the hymn had been extended by three stanzas and the benediction had been quietly pronounced. I waited on the front pew until he rose. He broke the silence plaintively: "I want to be a Christian." My pleasure was jolted by an unexpected twist in the moment when he added, "But I have a question. Can you be a Christian and not believe in eternal life?" Never having considered the possibility, but eager to keep this prize fish on the hook, I shrugged and said, "I think so— but why?" He explained a mental barrier which had shielded him from the faith: Christianity struck him as greedy, self-indulgent. He did not want to be a Christian so he could get in on the best deal on earth, so he could get solid gold reward points for his mortal travels; and he certainly did not want to get on the bus to heaven in order to escape the horrors of hell. "If I become a Christian, I want to do it because it is true, good, beautiful, and right, not because of what I will selfishly get out of it." Either my brain stumbled into some luck or the Spirit moved quickly, as I heard myself respond reasonably well: "Then yes, you certainly can be a Christian, and I applaud your wise approach. But I have a question for you: when you die, if God should surprise you with the gift of eternal life in which you haven't believed, will that be okay with you?" He nodded.

What is this eternal life, anyway? If we think we know a lot about the nature of eternal life, we are misguided. Heaven is a mystery. If we think good things about heaven, we know the reality will exceed our thoughts by a measure that will cause us to blush. The future, even our future with God, has a mysterious quality, which need not surprise us, as the future stubbornly stores up and then parcels out the unexpected. Hebrews speaks of faith as "the evidence of things not seen"—and what we cannot see is the future. And as much as we would choose to know the future, God is better than our choosing.

The Unknown Is the Mind's Greatest Need

Emily Dickinson is said to have written, "The unknown is the mind's greatest need and for it no one thinks to thank God."[2] We are uncomfortable with the unknown, but the unknown is our greatest need, because the unknown is beyond what we can manage; the unknown is the destination of our deepest longing. In America we are taught that we are free, that we choose the life we inhabit—but this is laughably, patently false. Look to the rear: do you notice that you did not choose the most important facts about your life? I did not choose my gender, my parents, my skin color, my nationality, my proclivity to disease. The deepest truth about me is given; the cards simply are dealt. Look to the front, down the road ahead: what do you think you see? My financial planner projects income, insurance, retirement benefits; a good husband and father is prepared for the future, right? I counsel married couples, and ask them what their lives will be like ten or fifty years from now. They paint a picture; they need a vision, right? The truth is (and if you don't believe me, sit through a handful of counseling sessions with me, or just pay attention to people you know), we make plans, we prepare—but the most important event that will happen in my life will be something for which I will be totally, overwhelmingly unprepared.

And we do not mean only those jarring tragedies, the punches in the gut that take the wind out of you, but also the good. The most beautiful gifts I have received were not planned, calculated, or anticipated. A tap on the shoulder, you turn, and a dream you never dreamed becomes reality. Of course, the painful, unanticipated interruption to life makes your knees buckle, and you cannot read any further, you cannot see the story going on or coming to any good end.

My wife reads murder mysteries; I hope she is not plotting to dispense with me. The marvel of these stories is the way events unfold, with various details making no apparent sense. She returned early from the market; he had red mud on his boots; a wine glass was broken on the floor; a towel is missing from the bathroom. What do these random, perhaps trivial, but then again perhaps crucial facts mean? We have no idea, or we think we have some idea, but then the detective steps into the circle of suspects and begins to piece the story together, explaining where she really went, why the mud was a huge clue, how the glass was shattered, where the towel was found. . . . We had been wondering: Could it be the maid? or the butler? or the lady of the house? But shock of all shocks: it was the gardener! Only at the end does the whole story make sense; only in light of the conclusion do the various little details, which yesterday seemed dull, strike us as so very important. "The sprawling, ramshackle narrative of events as lived by the characters is sprawling and ramshackle no more" (David Steinmetz).[3] Aristotle said that the mark of a good story is that as you are following it, you have no idea how it will end; but then when it ends, you realize it had to turn out that way.

Easter is akin to the narrator tipping us off on the end of the story. We stand in a circle, and Jesus steps out and explains it all. From the perspective of the end, everything else makes sense and finds its place. But with a difference. In the murder mysteries, the dead corpse stays cold. The widow goes home alone. The convicts wind up in jail. In the Gospel, the dead live, the widowed are reunited, the jails are emptied, the bars shattered—and we recognize that it had to turn out the way it will. And so we read our lives backwards, as Steinmetz says: "If one reads the last chapter first, one discovers a complex and intelligible narrative guided unerringly to its destined end by the secret hand of its author. Under the circumstances, reading backwards is not merely a preferred reading strategy; it is the only sensible course of action for a reasonable person."

Little Ones to Him Belong

On every vacation and even day outings, our family winds up in a cemetery, and we harbor a decided preference for nineteenth-century tombstones. They are stones, names, dates—but then stories begin to voice themselves in the silence, tales of heartbreak, extreme darkness. It is not hard to imagine young parents trudging up the hill with a small coffin, bearing a son who died after just three months. Then, the same father, numb with grief, mounts the same hill with a pair of coffins, this time a daughter, her birth having claimed the life of the mother in its gruesome train. We might expect the stones marking their place to curse God, to pronounce a verdict of nothingness. But instead we find poetry, Bible verses, or simple hymns, like the verse I once saw on three small stones, successive deaths of children under age five: "Little ones to him belong, they are weak, but he is strong."

We are weak, but he is strong. Before we can talk for one minute about our immortality, or being together in heaven, we had better

157

be sure that he is strong. Very strong. The Creed rises to its climax—
can you hear the massive chorus, the grand symphony, the clashing
cymbals?—as the God who was powerful enough fifteen billion
years ago to hurl the universe into being with a mere flick of the
divine wrist, who was powerful enough, loving enough to take on
human flesh, becoming vulnerable in the person of Jesus: this God
does not merely impress us and leave us slack-jawed. This God
draws us into the circle and bequeaths upon us an inheritance
beyond all imagining. All gift. All wonder. All good. Whatever frailty
we have suffered will be healed. Whatever unbearable agony we
have endured will be more than made right. Tears wiped away, no
more sorrow. Unfathomable beauty.

For now we hope. And we recall that there is a public, commu-
nal angle to eternal life. A friend and rabbi suggested to me what he
thought would be a difference between our faiths: "In Judaism
you're not saved as an individual; you're saved to be part of the
Jewish community; salvation is something we embrace together."
We misconstrue Christianity, however, if we think salvation is about
"me and Jesus, me and my eternal reward." As in Judaism, Christians
are saved to be part of the Church triumphant. You are saved so you
might find your place within the Body of Christ. We come to the
Lord's table, and we raise our voices in song, and we miss the point
if we think this is a nice religious activity. Gathering at the table,
singing the hymn: a vague but tantalizing glimpse into eternal life.
Out of our isolation, we are called together to share the one thing
that matters, the broken body and the shed blood of our Lord and
Savior, Jesus Christ. We find our place in Christ's family. We sing,
each voice distinct, but yet immersed in the great chorus of the
angels and saints, no soloists allowed, an ever-burgeoning cascade
of differing voices coalescing into a stunning, beautiful harmony of
praise.

Marching Orders

This is our destiny, our hope. And if we attend to the chorus, we
may detect, hidden in the gathering and song, marching orders. We
do not come to the table to sing, receive the grace of God, and
go back home as we normally would. We are energized, we are catapulted out into the world on a mission. Martin Luther King, Jr.,

speaking on behalf of Memphis garbage workers the night before he was assassinated, declared,

> It's all right to talk about long robes over yonder, in all of its symbolism, but ultimately people want some suits and dresses and shoes to wear down here. It's all right to talk about streets flowing with milk and honey, but God has commanded us to be concerned about the slums down here, and his children who can't eat three square meals a day. It's all right to talk about the new Jerusalem, but one day, God's preacher must talk about the new New York, the new Atlanta, the new Philadelphia, the new Los Angeles, the new Memphis.[4]

If we pray "Thy will be done on earth as it is in heaven," we would be wise to arrange this world as closely as we may to the world we long to inhabit for an inestimably long period of time, or really, when all the clocks and watches are thrown out, to be zealous champions down here of what the kingdom of God will look like up there, noticing to our surprise that "all the way to heaven is heaven" (Catherine of Siena).

At the end of the last *Lord of the Rings* film, *The Return of the King,* Pippin, distraught by the pains, sorrows, and looming defeat the Hobbits had suffered in their quest, turns to the wise old wizard Gandalf and says, "I never thought it would end like this." Gandalf unveils an alternative plot Pippin had not expected: "End? No. The journey doesn't end here. There's another path we all must take. The gray-rained curtain of this world rolls back and it will change to silver clouds, and then you see it. White shores and beyond a far green country under a swift sunrise." My brothers and sisters, Jesus is risen. This is our hope. This is the surprise. The universe turns on an unseen axis. The ending of the story is out. So I invite you to believe. Come and be part of the church, those who believe in the resurrection, those who trust not in themselves, but in God's great, glorious future surprise.

Notes

1. Mitch Albom, *The Five People You Meet in Heaven* (New York: Hyperion, 2003).
2. Quoted by William Sloane Coffin, *The Heart Is a Little to the Left: Essays on*

Public Morality (Hanover, N.H.: University Press of New England, 1999). Coffin quoted Dickinson to this effect often, but I have been unable to find the words in any collection of Dickinson's writing.

3. For this line of thought we are indebted to David C. Steinmetz, "Uncovering a Second Narrative: Detective Fiction and the Construction of Historical Method," *The Art of Reading Scripture,* ed. Ellen F. Davis and Richard B. Hays (Grand Rapids: Eerdmans, 2003), 54-65.

4. Martin Luther King, Jr., *A Testament of Hope: The Essential Writings and Speeches of Martin Luther King, Jr.,* ed. James Melvin Washington (San Francisco: HarperSanFrancisco, 1986), 282.

APPENDIX
WORSHIP AND MUSIC
RESOURCES

Selected by Kevin Turner

For the following appendix, hymns and praise choruses are listed first, followed by anthems. The hymns are listed with the following abbreviations signifying the resources:

(UM) *The United Methodist Hymnal*
(TFWS) *The Faith We Sing* (supplement to the *UM Hymnal*)
(PH) *Presbyterian Hymnal*
(EH) *The Hymnal 1982*—Hymnal of the Episcopal Church
(WLP) *Wonder, Love, and Praise: A Supplement to The Hymnal 1982*
(LBW) *Lutheran Book of Worship*

General Creed–based hymns (doxological in nature)

UM 61, PH 139, LBW 522, EH 365 "Come, Thou Almighty King" ITALIAN HYMN

UM 64, PH 138, LBW 165, EH 362 "Holy, Holy, Holy! Lord God Almighty" NICAEA

UM 79, PH 460, LBW 535, EH 366 "Holy God, We Praise Thy Name" GROSSER GOTT

UM 85 "We Believe in One True God" RATISBON

PH 137 "We All Believe in One True God" WIR GLAUBEN ALL AN EINEN GOTT

LBW 374 "We All Believe in One True God" WIR GLAUBEN ALL (different tune than in PH)

UM 98, PH 485 "To God Be the Glory" TO GOD BE THE GLORY (old-time favorite)

UM 99 "My Tribute" MY TRIBUTE (new favorite)

161

PH 523 "God the Spirit, Guide and Guardian" BETHANY

UM 648 "God the Spirit, Guide and Guardian" HYFRYDOL (different than in PH)

WLP 743 "O Threefold God of Tender Unity" FLENTGE

"I Believe in God, the Father Almighty"

Hymns and Choruses

UM 60, PH 253, EH 429 "I'll Praise My Maker While I've Breath" OLD 13TH

UM 66, PH 478, LBW 549, EH 410 "Praise, My Soul, the King of Heaven" LAUDA ANIMA

PH 479 "Praise, My Soul, the God of Heaven" (more ecumenical/gender neutral version)

UM 96 "Praise the Lord Who Reigns Above" AMSTERDAM

UM 115 "How Like a Gentle Spirit" SURSUM CORDA (male/female references; emphasis on God's Love)

UM 123 "El Shaddai" EL SHADDAI

TFWS 2023 "How Majestic Is Your Name" by Michael W. Smith HOW MAJESTIC

TFWS 2040 "Awesome God" by Rich Mullins (contemporary) AWESOME GOD

WLP 768, 769 "I believe in God Almighty" (Gaelic and Welsh melodies, respectively)

"Jehovah-Jireh" by Merla Watson, Catacombs Productions, Ltd.

"Ancient of Days" by Gary Sadler and Jamie Harvill, Integrity's Hosanna! Music/Integrity's Praise! Music

"For Your Name Is Holy" by Jim Cowan, Integrity's Hosanna Music

"Blessed Are You" by Donna Milgaten, Donna Milgaten Music and Jenai Publishing

"Blessed Be the Lord God Almighty" by Bob Fitts, Scripture in Song

"Lord (I Don't Know)" by Steve Taylor and Peter Furler, Ariose Music/Soylent Tunes

Anthems

One Faith, One Hope, One Lord. Craig Courtney. SATB, organ/opt.tpt. or brass qnt. Sacred Music Press S-462 (accessible harmonies to the listener)

One Faith. John-Michael Talbot. Birdwing Music (contemporary, folk-style melodies)

Heilig. Felix Mendelssohn-Bartholdy. ed. Ray Robinson. SATB (dbl choir) Hinshaw Music, Inc. HMC-1135 (difficult; in German with English translation)

"Maker of heaven and earth"

Hymns and Choruses

UM 92, PH 473, LBW 561 "For the Beauty of the Earth" DIX

EH 416 "For the Beauty of the Earth" LUCERNA DAUDONAIE

UM 144, PH 293, LBW 554 "This Is My Father's World" TERRA BEATA (PATRIS)

EH 651 "This Is My Father's World" MERCER STREET

PH 458, LBW 558, EH 412 "Earth and All Stars" DEXTER or EARTH AND ALL STARS

UM 89, PH 464, LBW 551, EH 376 "Joyful, Joyful, We Adore Thee" HYMN TO JOY

UM 97, PH 553, EH 424 "For the Fruit of This Creation" EAST ACKLAM

LBW 563 "For the Fruits of All Creation" SANTA BARBARA

UM 62, PH 455, LBW 527, EH 400 "All Creatures of Our God and King" LASST UNS ERFREUEN

UM 100 "God, Whose Love Is Reigning o'er Us" LAUDA ANIMA

UM 109 "Creating God, Your Fingers Trace" KEDRON

PH 134 "Creating God, Your Fingers Trace" HANCOCK

EH 394,395 "Creating God, Your Fingers Trace" WILDERNESS, KING (respectively)

UM 77, PH 467, LBW 532 "How Great Thou Art" HOW GREAT THOU ART (O STORE GUD)

UM 443 "O God Who Shaped Creation" TUOLUMNE

UM 145, PH 469, EH 8 "Morning Has Broken" BUNESSAN

UM 147, PH 267, EH 405 "All Things Bright and Beautiful" ROYAL OAK

PH 266 "Thank You, God, for Water, Soil, and Air" AMSTEIN

UM 148, PH 271, EH 385 "Many and Great, O God" (native American with drum ostinato) LACQUIPARLE

UM 149 "Cantemos al Señor" (Let's Sing unto the Lord) (Spanish hymn) ROSAS

UM 150, PH 268, LBW 463, EH 580 "God, Who Stretched the Spangled Heavens" HOLY MANNA

UM 604, LBW 191 "Praise and Thanksgiving Be to God" CHRISTE SANCTORUM

UM 728 "Come Sunday" ELLINGTON

PH 273 "O God the Creator" KASTAAK

PH 470, EH 48 "O Day of Radiant Gladness" ES FLOG EIN KLEINS WALDVÖGELEIN

UM 151, PH 290 "God Created Heaven and Earth" TOA-SIA (Taiwanese melody)

WLP 746, 747 "God the Sculptor of the Mountains" SANDRIA/URBS BEATA

TFWS 2060 "God the Sculptor of the Mountains" JENNINGS-HOUSTON

PH 285 "God, You Spin the Whirling Planets" AUSTRIAN HYMN

LBW 515 "How Marvelous God's Greatness" DEN BLOMSTERTID NU KOM-MER

"Ah, Lord God, Thou Hast Made the Heavens" by Kay Chance, Kay Chance c/o Dr. Heinrich, Jasper Str. 20, W-3353, Bad Gandersheim, Germany

"All Creation Worships You" by Kirk Dearman and Jim Mills, Integrity's Hosanna! Music

"Come and Worship" by Don Moen, Integrity's Hosanna Music

"The Lord Reigns" by Dan Stradwick, Scripture in Song (division of Integrity Music)

Anthems

All Things Bright and Beautiful. John Rutter. two-part choir arr. keyboard Hinshaw Music HMC 663 (SATB available)

O Praise the Lord of Heaven. William Billings. ed. Karl Kroeger. SATB, a cappella. Alliance Music Publishers AMP 0193

For the Beauty of the Earth. John Rutter. SATB, keyboard. Hinshaw Music HMC 550

Song of Exaltation. John Ness Beck. SATB, organ. Hal Leonard HL 50313920 (slow and fast parts-challenging rhythm)

The Heavens Are Telling from Creation. Franz J. Haydn. SATB, keyboard. Theodore Presser 332-00813

"And in Jesus Christ, his only son, our Lord"

Hymns and Choruses

UM 189, PH 306, EH 383, 384 "Fairest Lord Jesus" ST. ELIZABETH (also CURSADERS' HYMN)

LBW 518 "Beautiful Savior" SCHÖNSTER HERR JESU
TFWS 2071 "Jesus, Name above All Names" NAME ABOVE ALL NAMES
UM 173, PH 462, LBW 265 "Christ, Whose Glory Fills the Skies"
RATISBON
EH 6 "Christ, Whose Glory Fills the Skies" CHRIST WHOSE GLORY
UM 188 "Christ Is the World's Light" ST. ELIZABETH
EH 542 "Christ Is the World's True Light" ST. JOAN
UM 154, PH 142, LBW 328, EH 450 "All Hail the Power of Jesus'
Name" CORONATION
UM 155, PH 143 "All Hail the Power of Jesus' Name" CORONATION
LBW 329, EH 451 "All Hail the Power of Jesus' Name!" MILES LANE
TFWS 2069 "All Hail King Jesus" KING JESUS (chorus by Dave Moody)
UM 168, PH 148, LBW 179, EH 435 "At the Name of Jesus" KING'S
WESTON
"Jesus, Name Above All Names" by Naida Hearn, Scripture in Song
"Joy of My Desire" by Jennifer Randolph, Integrity's Hosanna! Music
"Jesus, All For Jesus" by Robin Mark, Word's Spirit of Praise Music
(administered by Maranatha! Music)

Anthems

God So Loved the World from *Crucifixion*. John Stainer. SATB, a cappella. Hal Leonard HL 50294340

God So Loved the World from *Crucifixion*. John Stainer/arr. Benjamin Harlan. SATB, keyboard. Hal Leonard
HL 08742558 (easier arrangement of Stainer with piano accompaniment)

Rejoice, the Lord Is King. Malcolm Archer. Kevin Mayhew, Ltd. (MelBay) 97964A

Beautiful Savior. arr. F. Melius Christiansen. SATB divisi, A solo. Augsburg Fortress 11-0051 (stunning arrangement for choir, strophic setting)

How Lovely Are the Messengers. Felix Mendelssohn-Bartholdy. SATB with keyboard. Carl Fischer CM620 (contains chorale "O Morning Star, How Fair and Bright!")

"Who was conceived by the Holy Spirit, born of the Virgin Mary"

Hymns and Choruses

UM 182 "Word of God, Come Down on Earth" LIEBSTER JESU
EH 633 "Word of God, Come Down on Earth" MT ST ALBAN NCA

PH 54, LBW 51, EH 80 "From Heaven Above to Earth I Come" VOM
HIMMEL HOCH

UM 184, PH 309, EH 82 "Of the Father's Love Begotten" DIVINUM
MYSTERIUM

UM 347 "Spirit Song" SPIRIT SONG

TFWS 2085 "He Came Down" HE CAME DOWN (traditional Cameroon
melody)

UM 598, PH 327, LBW 231, EH 632 "O Word [Christ] of God
Incarnate" MUNICH (MEININGEN)

UM 204 "Emmanuel, Emmanuel" MCGEE

"O Come Let Us Adore Him" arr. Teri Bryant and Matt Redman,
Thankyou Music (administered by worshiptogether.com Songs)

"Come, Emmanuel" by Twila Paris, Ariose Music/Mountain Spring
Music (EMI Christian Music Publishing)

"Adoration" by Steve Taylor and Peter Furler, Ariose Music/Soylent
Tunes (EMI Christian Music Publishing)

"Let All Mortal Flesh Keep Silence" arr. Fernando Ortega and John
Andrew Schreiner, Word Music

Anthems

Ave Maria. Franz Biebl. Hinshaw Music (three different arrange-
ments SSAATTBB HMC-1251, TTBB HMC-1253, and SATB with
SATB quartet HMC-1255) in Latin, beautiful harmonies; favorite of
congregations

Salvation Is Created, Paul Tschesnokoff. SAATTBB, a cappella.
J. Fischer and Bro/CPP/Belwin 4129-2½

A New Magnificat. Carolyn Jennings. SATB with congregation
response. Augsburg Fortress 11-10479 (contrasts Song of Mary
with Song of Hannah, includes congregational response; very
easy) also SAB version 11-2098

Veni Emmanuel from *Emmanuel-God With Us* (3 Advent anthems).
Robert H. Young. SATB divisi, a cappella. Plymouth Music Co, Inc.
PJMS-100

"Suffered under Pontius Pilate, was crucified, dead, and buried"

Hymns and Choruses

UM 285 "To Mock Your Reign, O Dearest Lord" KINGSFOLD

EH 170 "To Mock Your Reign, O Dearest Lord" THE THIRD TUNE
(Thomas Tallis)

UM 290, PH 97, LBW 109, EH 171 "Go to Dark Gethsemane" RED-HEAD (also GETHSEMANE or PETRA)

UM 286, PH 98, LBW 116, 117, EH 168, 169 "O Sacred Head, Now Wounded" PASSION CHORALE (HERZLICH TUT MICH VERLANGEN)

WLP 735 "O Sacred Head, Sore Wounded" by David Hurd

TFWS 2111 "We Sang Our Glad Hosannas" HOLY WEEK

UM 289, PH 93, LBW 123, EH 158 "Ah, Holy Jesus" HERZLIEBSTER JESU

TFWS 2113 "Lamb of God" by Twila Paris SWEET LAMB OF GOD

UM 288, PH 102, LBW 92, EH 172 "Were You There" WERE YOU THERE

"How Deep the Father's Love For Us" by Stuart Townend, Thankyou Music (administered by worshiptogether.com Songs)

"Lost in Wonder (You Chose the Cross)" by Martyn Layzell, Thankyou Music (administered by worshiptogether.com Songs)

"Above All" by Lenny LeBlanc and Paul Baloche, Integrity's Hosanna! Music & LenSongs Publishing

"Amazing Love" by Graham Kendrick, Make Way Music Integrity's Hosanna! Music

Anthems

Every Time I Think about Jesus. arr. L.L, Fleming. SATB. Augsburg Fortress 11-0539 (slow, mournful but powerful piece)

Crucifixus from *B minor Mass.* (simple, polyphonic Latin setting of the text) J. S. Bach. SATB. E. C. Shirmer 1174

Greater Love hath no man. John Ireland. SATB, B solo, organ. Galaxy 1.5030.1 (text from numerous portions of Scripture, colorful organ accompaniment)

When I Survey the Wondrous Cross. arr. Gilbert Martin. SATB, organ. Theodore Presser 312-40785

Agnus Dei from *Missa Festiva.* John Leavitt. SATB, piano. Warner Bros. SV 9007 (in Latin, but easy harmonies with simple piano accompaniment) also available in SSA and SAB

Solus ad victimam. Kenneth Leighton. SATB, organ. Oxford University Press A 309 (in English, sounds difficult, but very easy and powerful ending)

"The third day he rose from the dead"

Hymns and Choruses

UM 162, PH 106, EH 178 "Alleluia, Alleluia! Give Thanks to the Risen Lord" ALLELUIA NO. 1

167

UM 302 "Christ the Lord Is Risen Today" EASTER HYMN
PH 123, LBW 151, EH 207 "Jesus Christ Is Risen Today" EASTER HYMN
PH 113, LBW 128 "Christ the Lord Is Risen Today" LLANFAIR
LBW 130 "Christ the Lord Is Risen Today" (NO ALLELUIA) ORIENTIS
PARTIBUS
PH 112 "Christ the Lord Is Risen Today" CHRIST IST ERSTANDEN
UM 304 "Easter People, Raise Your Voices" REGENT SQUARE
UM 306, PH 119, LBW 135, EH 208 "The Strife Is O'er, the Battle
Done" VICTORY
UM 310 "He Lives" ACKLEY
TFWS 2115 "Christ Has Risen" HOLY MANNA
TFWS 2116 "Christ the Lord Is Risen" GARU (Ghanian folk song)
"Jesus Is Alive" by Ron Kenoly, Integrity's Hosanna! Music
"Crowned With Many Crowns" by Gary Sadler, Integrity's Hosanna!
Music
"I Believe in Jesus" by Marc Nelson, Mercy Publishing/adm. by
Music Services
"Redeemer, Savior, Friend" by Darrell Evans and Chris Springer,
Integrity's Hosanna! Music
"Only Jesus" by John Chisum, Integrity's Hosanna! Music
"Celebrate Jesus" by Gary Oliver, Integrity's Hosanna! Music

Anthems

On the Third Day. Allen Pote. SATB, keyboard, brass, and handbells.
Hope Publishing Co. F 1000 (easy anthem; SAB also available
Hope Publishing C-5124)
Credo from *Gospel Mass.* Robert Ray. SATB, piano, drums, bass gui-
tar. Jenson Publishing/Hal Leonard Corporation 8740901 (literal
setting of the Apostles' Creed with some extra stories thrown in;
gospel piece with solos)
Easter Anthem. William Billings arr. Shaw. SATB, a cappella. G.
Schirmer 9949 (early American composer)
Ye Choirs of New Jerusalem. C. V. Stanford. SATB. Organ. GIA G-4188
(challenging for both choir and organ)
Easter Morning. Paul J. Christiansen. SATB. Augsburg Fortress 11-
1057 (sweet setting of the Easter garden story)

*"He ascended into heaven and sitteth at the right hand of God the
Father Almighty; from thence he shall come to judge the quick and
the dead."*

Hymns and Choruses

LBW 158, EH 460, 461 "Alleluia! Sing to Jesus" HYFRYDOL or ALLELUIA

UM 312, EH 214 "Hail the Day That Sees Him Rise" LLANFAIR

UM 327, PH 151, LBW 170, EH 494 "Crown Him with Many Crowns" DIADEMATA

UM 176 "Majesty, Worship His Majesty" MAJESTY

PH 180 "The God of Heaven" GLORY (newer hymn in 4 with irregular syllabic meter)

UM 324, PH 120, LBW 142, EH 216 "Hail Thee, Festival Day!" SALVE FESTA DIES

UM 157, PH 423, LBW 530, EH 544 "Jesus Shall Reign" DUKE STREET

"Lion of Judah" by Robin Mark, Daybreak Music, Ltd. (administered by Integrity's Hosanna! Music)

"Let God Arise" by John Sellers, Integrity's Hosanna! Music

"Beautiful One" by Tim Hughes, Thankyou Music (administered by worshiptogether.com Songs)

"Clap, Clap Your Hands" by Jennifer Randolph, Integrity's Hosanna Music

"Clap Your Hands" by Charlie LeBlanc, Integrity's Hosanna! Music

"Come and Worship" by Don Moen, Integrity's Hosanna! Music

"He Reigns" by Peter Furler and Steve Taylor, Ariose Music (adm. by EMI Christian Publishing)/Soylent Tunes

Anthems

O Clap Your Hands. John Rutter. SATB, organ. Oxford University Press A307 (complicated and rhythmic anthem with organ)

God Is Gone Up. Gerald Finzi. SATB divisi. Organ. Boosey and Hawkes OCTB1926 (extended work with demanding organ part)

God Is Gone Up With A Merry Noise. John Leavitt. SATB. Concordia Publishing House CPH 98-3649 (more contemporary setting with brass)

God Has Gone Up with a Shout (#11 of *Acclamations Set 2*). Hal Hopson. SATB, handbells. Sacred Music Press S531

O Clap Your Hands. Ralph Vaughan Williams. SATB divisi, organ or brass. Galaxy Music/E.C. Shirmer Catalog No. 1.5000 (big work that ends even bigger)

"I believe in the Holy Spirit"

Hymns and Choruses

UM 604 "Praise and Thanksgiving Be to God" CHRISTE SANCTORUM

PH 321 "Holy Spirit, Truth Divine" SONG 13

PH 472, WLP 786 "Cantad al Señor" (O Sing to the Lord) (Brazilian hymn)

UM 539 "O Spirit of the Living God" FOREST GREEN

UM 603 "Come, Holy Ghost, Our Hearts Inspire" WINCHESTER OLD

EH 507 "Praise the Spirit in Creation" JULION

TFWS 2117 "Spirit of God" DOVE SONG

PH 126, EH 510 "Come, Holy Spirit, Heavenly Dove" ST. AGNES

UM 651, PH 125, LBW 472, 473, EH 504 "Come, Holy Spirit, Our Souls Inspire" VENI CREATOR (SPIRITUS)

UM 393, PH 322 "Spirit of the Living God" LIVING GOD

"Consuming Fire" by Tim Hughes, Thankyou Music (adm. by www. worshiptogether.com Songs)

"Breathe on Me" by Lucy Fisher, Lucy Fisher/Hillsongs Australia (administered by Integrity's Hosanna! Music)

"I Hear Music" by David Baroni, Intergrity's Praise! Music

"Spirit of the Living God" by Pete Sanchez, Jr., Integrity's Hosanna! Music

"Let Your Spirit Rise Within Me" by Randy Spier, Integrity's Hosanna! Music

Anthems

Gracious Spirit, Dwell With Me. K. Lee Scott. 2-part, keyboard. Augsburg Fortress 11-2198 (easy 2-part mixed anthem)

Veni, Creator Spiritus. Richard Marlow. Double Mixed Choir, S solo. Oxford University Press RSCM CMS010 (Latin and English/ challenging)

All That Hath Life And Breath Praise Ye The Lord. René Clausen. SATB divisi, a cappella. Mark Foster MF223 (Psalms 96 and 22; clever portrayal of speaking in tongues)

Hymn to the Holy Spirit. Randolph Currie. SATB, organ. GIA G-2962 (easier anthem, but difficult with chant rhythms)

"The holy catholic church, the communion of saints, the forgiveness of sins"

Hymns and Choruses

UM 604, LBW 191 "Praise and Thanksgiving Be to God" CHRISTE SANC-
TORUM

UM 79, PH 460, LBW 535, EH 366 "Holy God, We Praise Thy Name"
GROSSER GOTT

UM 547 "O Church of God, United" ELLACOMBE

UM 557, PH 438, LBW 370 "Blest Be the Tie That Binds" DENNIS

UM 545, 546, PH 442, LBW 369, EH 525 "The Church's One
Foundation" AURELIA

UM 712, PH 364, EH 293 "I Sing a Song of the Saints of God" GRAND
ISLE

UM 702 "Sing with All the Saints in Glory" HYMN TO JOY

UM 706 "Soon and Very Soon" (short song, repeated song) VERY SOON

UM 708 "Rejoice in God's Saints" HANOVER

UM 709 "Come, Let Us Join Our Friends Above" FOREST GREEN

LBW 254 "Come, Let Us Join Our Cheerful Songs" NUN DANKET ALL

PH 181 "Come Sing to God" ELLACOMBE

UM 711, PH 526, LBW 174, EH 287 "For All the Saints" SINE NOMINE

"How Deep the Father's Love For Us" by Stuart Townend, Thankyou
Music (administered by worshiptogether.com Songs)

"Glory and Honor" by Twila Paris, Ariose Music/Mountain Spring
Music

"Come, Ye Sinners, Poor and Needy" arr. Fernando Ortega and John
Andrew Schreiner, Word Music (duet)

"We Have Overcome" by Ed Kerr and Steve Merkel, Integrity's
Hosanna! Music

"Sing to the King" by Billy James Foote (uses 1st stanza and theme
from Sing We the King by Charles Silvester Horne, 1910), www.
worshiptogether.com/sixsteps music

Anthems

One Faith. John-Michael Talbot. 1988 Birdwing Music (contemporary, folk-style melodies)

Hark, I hear the harps eternal. arr. Shaw-Parker. SATB, a cappella.
Lawson-Gould/Warner Bros. LG51331

Bright Canaan. arr. Shaw-Parker. SATB, a cappella. Lawson-
Gould/Warner Bros. LG 00919 (accessible to small choirs)

They Are at Rest. Edward Elgar. SATB, a cappella. Collegium CCS 202 (very chromatic and expressive)

Souls of the Righteous. T. Tertius Noble/arr. Hal Hopson. SATB, organ. Hinshaw Music HMC-1437 (text from Apocrypha)

"The resurrection of the body, and the life everlasting"

Hymns and Choruses

UM 724 "On Jordan's Stormy Banks I Stand" PROMISED LAND

UM 728 "Come Sunday" ELLINGTON

UM 701 "When We All Get to Heaven" HEAVEN

UM 707 "Hymn of Promise" PROMISE

UM 60, PH 253, EH 429 "I'll Praise My Maker While I've Breath" OLD 113TH

UM 528 "Nearer, My God, to Thee" BETHANY

UM 303, PH 118 "The Day of Resurrection" LANCASHIRE

LBW 141 "The Day of Resurrection!" HERZLICH TUT MICH ERFREUEN

EH 210 "The Day of Resurrection!" ELLACOMBE

UM 723 "Shall We Gather At the River" HANSON PLACE

UM 557, PH 438, LBW 370 "Blest Be the Tie That Binds" DENNIS

UM 703 "Swing Low, Sweet Chariot" SWING LOW

TFWS 2282 "I'll Fly Away" I'LL FLY AWAY

"When It's All Been Said and Done" by Jim Cowan, Integrity's Hosanna! Music

"You Are the One I Love" by Lenny LeBlanc, Integrity's Hosanna! Music and LenSongs Publishing

"Take Me In" by Dave Browning, Glory Alleluia Music (administered by Tempo Publications, Inc.)

"On the Road to Beautiful" by Charlie Hall, worshiptogether.com Songs/sixsteps music

Anthems

And I Saw a New Heaven. Edgar Bainton. SATB, organ. Novello and Co. 29 0342 03 (beautiful English cathedral anthem portraying eternity)

At the River. Aaron Copland arr. R Wilding White. SATB, piano. Boosey and Hawkes OCTB 5513 (also available in SSA OCTB-5512 and TTBB OCTB 5514)

Eternal Life. Olive Dungan/ arr. William Stickles. SATB, piano. Theodore Presser 322-40018 (choral setting of this Prayer of St. Francis)

Swing Low, Sweet Chariot. arr. Shaw-Parker. SATB, T solo. Lawson Gould/Warner Bros. LG00984 (beautiful, serene setting of this favorite)

Made in the USA
Lexington, KY
12 July 2016